D0844719

Modern Critical Interpretations

Anthony Trollope's
Barchester Towers and The Warden

Modern Critical Interpretations

These and other titles in preparation

Anthony Trollope's
Barchester Towers
and The Warden

Edited and with an introduction by

Harold Bloom
Sterling Professor of the Humanities
Yale University

Chelsea House Publishers ◊ *1988*

NEW YORK ◊ NEW HAVEN ◊ PHILADELPHIA

© 1988 by Chelsea House Publishers, a division
of Chelsea House Educational Communications, Inc.

Introduction © 1988 by Harold Bloom

Printed and bound in the United States of America

10   9   8   7   6   5   4   3   2   1

∞ The paper used in this publication meets the minimum
requirements of the American National Standard for
Permanence of Paper for Printed Library Materials, Z39.48–1984.

Library of Congress Cataloging-in-Publication Data
Anthony Trollope's Barchester Towers and The warden.
    (Modern critical interpretations)
    Bibliography: p.
    Includes index.
    1. Trollope, Anthony, 1815–1882.   Barchester Towers.
2. Trollope, Anthony, 1815–1882.   The warden.
I. Bloom, Harold.   II. Series.
PR5684.B36A82   1988   823'.8   87-27654
ISBN 0-87754-748-3

Contents

Editor's Note

This book brings together a representative selection of the best modern critical interpretations of two related and superb novels by Anthony Trollope, *The Warden* (1855) and *Barchester Towers* (1857), his first successful works and the inaugural volumes in his great cycle *Chronicles of Barsetshire*. The critical essays are reprinted here in the chronological order of their original publication. I am grateful to Marena Fisher for her erudite aid in editing this volume.

My introduction, on *Barchester Towers*, centers on the confrontation between Bertie Stanhope and Mrs. Proudie after the great sofa fiasco. Sherman Hawkins begins the chronological sequence of criticism with his classic examination of Trollope's ambivalent view of the Established Church in *The Warden*, the positive aspect of which is expressed in the lonely and gentle heroism of Mr. Harding. *The Warden* is analyzed also by Hugh L. Hennedy as a novel centered upon the authentic vocation manifested by Mr. Harding.

U. C. Knoepflmacher reads *Barchester Towers* as Trollope's comic reaction to a changing England that has rendered his characters archaic, since they reflect an earlier social and cultural reality. In a subtle exegesis, James R. Kincaid studies both *The Warden* and *Barchester Towers* as Trollope's versions of pastoral, with Mr. Harding as hero.

P. D. Edwards, defining the psychic boundaries or limits of Trollope's Barset, cunningly reads the Bertie Stanhope–Mrs. Proudie sofa catastrophe as a concealed sexual confrontation. In the view of Robert M. Polhemus, the comedy of *Barchester Towers* is a serious reformation of its characters' personality and behavior in order to accommodate profound disruptions in personal and social existence.

Andrew Wright emphasizes that *Barchester Towers* is not a study of the nostalgias, but a sharply benign depiction of "an unlovely struggle." To Robin Gilmour, the novel's challenge by history is met by Trollope's originality; he is neither conservative nor reformer, but a personalist, concerned for the individual sensibility of his protagonists. In this volume's final essay, Christopher Herbert argues that *Barchester Towers* is part of Trollope's subversive program for correcting his era's repressive morality by asserting the claims of comic pleasure, in the novel as in life.

Introduction

The Warden and *Barchester Towers* are very different novels, but forever linked by continuities of composition, context, and personages. Unlike *The Warden*, *Barchester Towers* essentially is a comic novel. Trollope is hardly a novelist whom we can characterize in simple terms, because there are wholly equivocal elements in his narrative art. He can be very funny indeed and I agree with Christopher Herbert's contention that Trollope subtly dissented from his era's overt deprecation of fleshly and worldly pleasures. But Trollope was scarcely a hedonist or a vitalist and his dissent was limited; not half-hearted, but rhetorically muted. You have to read him with an intense awareness of tone, as Herbert does, in order to hear his comic endorsement of desire and to apprehend that he is not a sentimentalist in the ostensible religion of married love that is generally imposed upon him. Herbert persuades me, as against the views of such critics as J. Hillis Miller and Walter M. Kendrick, who threaten unwittingly to drown Trollope in a bathos he himself had fought against. Yet there is a missing quality in Trollope, a zest or gusto that would recommend his more interesting immoralists to us unreservedly.

C. P. Snow remarked that Trollope was "both skeptical and secretive and it seems not unlikely that, alone with himself, he came to believe rather little." That is convincing to me, since neither the theology nor the national church politics of *The Warden* and *Barchester Towers* greatly concern Trollope, whose interest is rather in the agon of personalities. Novels, as everyone agrees, trade in morals and manners, but the puzzle of Trollope is that we never quite can establish his stance as a moralist, if only because it is more evasive and more personal than it presents itself as being. Snow usefully reminds us that, a decade after *Barchester Towers*, Trollope stood as a

1

Liberal candidate for Parliament, a venture consonant with lifelong Whiggish sympathies on Trollope's part. In *Barchester Towers*, Trollope clearly favors the Tory, High Church group of the archdeacon and his friends over the Liberal Evangelicals: Bishop Proudie, the haughty Mrs. Proudie, the reprehensible chaplain Slope. Snow calls this a crossing of Trollope's vote, but I suppose instead we might call this Trollope's own version of comic realism, inherited by him from his master, Thackeray. More than Thackeray, Trollope seems to know implicitly that "comic realism" is a kind of oxymoron. Jacobean comedy, which Herbert demonstrates to be one of Trollope's prime sources, can be quite phantasmagoric, if not as wildly so as Jacobean tragedy. Fletcher, Massinger, and Middleton at once excited Trollope's overt moral disapproval and his deeper interest, since Fletcher in particular was a quarry for Trollope, as Herbert observes:

> It is easy to extract from Trollope's annotations a typical Victorian condemnation of the vein of sexual scandal that runs through comedy; Jeremy Collier himself was hardly more indignant than Trollope at the pervading immorality of the comic stage. Yet major qualifications must at once be made to such a comparison. For one thing, Trollope constantly declares that even the smuttiest and most "disgusting" comedies, such as Beaumont's and Fletcher's *The Knight of Malta* or Fletcher's *A Wife for a Month*, are in fact highly entertaining in spite of themselves. He condemns the bawdy-tongued heroines of Fletcher's *The Wild-Goose-Chase*, then praises this superlative comedy as "an excellent play, full of wit, with much language almost worthy of Shakespeare." The various characters, he says, "are kept up with such infinite life that the piece is charming to read, and must have charmed when acted"— an equation of "charm" with "life," incidentally, that goes to the heart of our theme. Divided judgments like these highlight the obvious paradox in the spectacle of a prudish Victorian moralist who endlessly describes himself as disgusted and repelled by Jacobean comedy, yet who reads it almost insatiably for decades, and shows, indeed, a special fascination for the very playwright he condemns most strongly for his lewdness (for Trollope read Fletcher's

huge body of work twice, first in the early 1850s—this being the only reading project recorded for these dates—then again from 1869 to 1874). One need not be a Freudian analyst to draw the conclusion that Trollope was keenly attracted to the "indecency" of comedy and to the enfranchisement it offered from the straitjacket of the Victorian cult of sexual purity, particularly with reference to women. His fulminations against it, we may assume, are in direct proportion to his instinctive attraction toward it.

The oddest aspect of Trollope in this matter is that he himself augments the repression, beyond even the call of his society, and then the repressed returns in him, with necessarily greater force. I would revise Herbert only to that degree; Trollope is far more prudish than his precursor Thackeray and subsequently he exceeds Thackeray in subverting societal expectations. Since Trollope, however, had internalized those expectations, he necessarily subverts himself. Such a narrative process is considerably more difficult to apprehend than is Thackeray's ambivalent stance, which at once satirizes Vanity Fair yet also stays well within it. There is a repressed Jacobean vitalist in Trollope, but mostly he maintained the repression.

Barchester Towers is a social comedy whose realism is consistent if a little uneasy. Kafka partly derived from Dickens, monumental fantasist; we could not envision Kafka reading, and being influenced by, Trollope. Yet Trollope's most surprising talent is his inventiveness, which can be simultaneously outrageous and persuasive, like social reality itself. The glory of *Barchester Towers*, and my own favorite moment in Victorian fiction, is the superb apotheosis at Mrs. Proudie's reception, when the astonishing Bertie Stanhope propels the sofa of his invalid sister, the grand vamp La Signora Madeline Vesey Neroni, on its epic voyage into the proud torso of Mrs. Proudie:

> "They've got this sofa into the worst possible part of the room; suppose we move it. Take care, Madeline."
>
> The sofa had certainly been so placed that those who were behind it found great difficulty in getting out; there was but a narrow gangway, which one person could stop. This was a bad arrangement, and one which Bertie thought it might be well to improve.

"Take care, Madeline," said he, and turning to the fat rector, added, "Just help me with a slight push."

The rector's weight was resting on the sofa and unwittingly lent all its impetus to accelerate and increase the motion which Bertie intentionally originated. The sofa rushed from its moorings and ran half-way into the middle of the room. Mrs. Proudie was standing with Mr. Slope in front of the signora, and had been trying to be condescending and sociable; but she was not in the very best of tempers, for she found that, whenever she spoke to the lady, the lady replied by speaking to Mr. Slope. Mr. Slope was a favourite, no doubt, but Mrs. Proudie had no idea of being less thought of than the chaplain. She was beginning to be stately, stiff, and offended, when unfortunately the castor of the sofa caught itself in her lace train and carried away there is no saying how much of her garniture. Gathers were heard to go, stitches to crack, plaits to fly open, flounces were seen to fall, and breadths to expose themselves; a long ruin of rent lace disfigured the carpet and still clung to the vile wheel on which the sofa moved.

So, when a granite battery is raised, excellent to the eyes of warfaring men, is its strength and symmetry admired. It is the work of years. Its neat embrasures, its finished parapets, its casemated stories show all the skill of modern science. But, anon, a small spark is applied to the treacherous fusee—a cloud of dust arises to the heavens—and then nothing is to be seen but dirt and dust and ugly fragments.

We know what was the wrath of Juno when her beauty was despised. We know to what storms of passion even celestial minds can yield. As Juno may have looked at Paris on Mount Ida, so did Mrs. Proudie look on Ethelbert Stanhope when he pushed the leg of the sofa into her lace train.

"Oh, you idiot, Bertie!" said the signora, seeing what had been done and what were to be the consequences.

"Idiot!" re-echoed Mrs. Proudie, as though the word were not half strong enough to express the required meaning; "I'll let him know—" and then looking round to learn, at a glance, the worst, she saw that at present it behoved her to collect the scattered *débris* of her dress.

Bertie, when he saw what he had done, rushed over the sofa and threw himself on one knee before the offended lady. His object, doubtless, was to liberate the torn lace from the castor, but he looked as though he were imploring pardon from a goddess.

"Unhand it, sir!" said Mrs. Proudie. From what scrap of dramatic poetry she had extracted the word cannot be said, but it must have rested on her memory and now seemed opportunely dignified for the occasion.

"I'll fly to the looms of the fairies to repair the damage, if you'll only forgive me," said Ethelbert, still on his knees.

"Unhand it, sir!" said Mrs. Proudie with redoubled emphasis and all but furious wrath. This allusion to the fairies was a direct mockery and intended to turn her into ridicule. So at least it seemed to her. "Unhand it, sir!" she almost screamed.

"It's not me; it's the cursed sofa," said Bertie, looking imploringly in her face and holding up both his hands to show that he was not touching her belongings, but still remaining on his knees.

Hereupon the signora laughed; not loud, indeed, but yet audibly. And as the tigress bereft of her young will turn with equal anger on any within reach, so did Mrs. Proudie turn upon her female guest.

"Madam!" she said—and it is beyond the power of prose to tell of the fire which flashed from her eyes.

The signora stared her full in the face for a moment, and then turning to her brother said playfully, "Bertie, you idiot, get up."

By this time the bishop, and Mr. Slope, and her three daughters were around her, and had collected together the wide ruins of her magnificence. The girls fell into circular rank behind their mother, and thus following her and carrying out the fragments, they left the reception-rooms in a manner not altogether devoid of dignity. Mrs. Proudie had to retire and re-array herself.

As soon as the constellation had swept by, Ethelbert

rose from his knees and, turning with mock anger to the fat rector, said: "After all it was your doing, sir—not mine. But perhaps you are waiting for preferment, and so I bore it."

Were I the New Longinus, composing *Upon Strong Writing* or *On the New Sublime*, I would employ this as one of the greatest comic scenes in literature, when read within its full context in *Barchester Towers*. Trollope somewhere declares that "the sublime may be mingled with the realistic, if the writer has the power." The creator of Bertie Stanhope—who cheerfully has failed at every possible and improbable career: the Anglican Church, the law, English and German universities, painter in Rome, the Jesuits, Jewish convert in Palestine, sculptor in Carrara, but who remains an absolute original—now gives that creation his finest moment, in the sofa debacle. The comparison of Mrs. Proudie's dress to the granite battery is merely perfect, since dress and granite contain the same entity, aggressive and hostile. The threefold "Unhand it, sir!" will not be matched for forty years, until Wilde's Lady Bracknell commands Jack: "Rise, sir, from this semi-recumbent posture," in one of the few literary works until the early Evelyn Waugh that might be worthy of accommodating Bertie Stanhope. But neither Wilde nor Waugh has anything like the military or naval maneuver in which the Proudie girls "fell into circular rank behind their mother, and thus following her and carrying out the fragments, they left the reception-rooms in a manner not altogether devoid of dignity." Trollope's triumph, more original than we now can realize, has had many imitators since, but this mode of comic disaster remains very much his own.

Mr. Harding's Church Music

Sherman Hawkins

The Warden, perhaps the most perfectly integrated of the Barchester novels, is the product of a divided mind. The clamor of ecclesiastical reformers against the misuse of endowments at Rochester and St. Cross evoked in Trollope strong and contradictory reactions. No other work, he tells us, ever took up so much of his thoughts. He was struck by two "opposite evils," "the possession by the Church of certain funds and endowments which had been intended for charitable purposes, but which had been allowed to become incomes for idle Church dignitaries," and "the undeserved severity of the newspapers towards the recipients of such incomes, who could hardly be considered to be the chief sinners in the matter." The product of these opposing attitudes is the Reverend Septimus Harding, warden of the pauper's hospital in Barchester, an "idle Church dignitary" who decides he has no moral right to his income and resigns his post.

In his *Autobiography*, Trollope declared that he was wrong in attempting to combine both points of view. He should have chosen one side and clung to that: "There should be no scruple of conscience." He might, for instance, have described "a bloated parson, with a red nose and every iniquity . . . living riotously on funds purloined from the poor." But *The Warden* itself turns upon "scruples of conscience," and when he wrote it, Trollope understood

From *ELH* 29, no. 2 (June 1962). © 1962 by the Johns Hopkins University Press, Baltimore/London.

his function very differently. The parodies of Carlyle and Dickens in chapter 15 suggest Trollope's conception of his method and subject. For "Dr. Pessimist Anticant," the abuse of the Hospital Funds simply evidences the "decay of the world," the degeneration of "all things in these modern days." True to Carlyle's method and philosophy, he shows this decline by contrasted individuals: John Hiram, founder of the Hospital, and Mr. Harding, his modern representative, the "godly man" of today and long ago. But the real villain is history: this is what the present makes of the past. For "Mr. Popular Sentiment," on the other hand, the corruption of the hospital results from pure human malignancy. In his novel, we find an authentic Dickensian villain, a clerical "demon," none other than the red-nosed monster of the *Autobiography*. Of course, both points of view are absurdly one-sided. The relations of past and present, of human good and evil are more complex, since "in this world no good is unalloyed, and . . . there is but little evil that has not in it some seed of what is goodly." The social novelist is neither prophet nor propagandist. He must show both sides: latter-day pamphlets and moral melodramas can only simplify the real issues of reform. Yet their very simplifications help define these issues. How is an institutional religion to preserve its original meaning through the centuries? How can the "godlike work" of its founder be carried on in modern times? No matter how divine its origin, it ultimately passes into the hands of professional churchmen like Mr. Harding or his son-in-law, Dr. Grantly. What becomes of a religion administered and represented by such very human men as these? The parodies of Anticant and Sentiment suggest problems of continuity and human fallibility central, in any Protestant view, to institutional religion. For the true subject of *The Warden* is the Church, and the paradoxes and problems which arise when an impulse of the spirit must be translated into a corporation with a bank account.

Trollope's ambivalent view of the Church is obvious in *Clergymen of the Church of England* (1866). Here his affection for the picturesque traditional order is balanced by ironic attacks on its "sweet mediaeval flavour of Old English corruption." Several of the chapters are built on a contrast of old and new, and the theme of the book is change. "We are often told that ours is a utilitarian age, but this utilitarian spirit is so closely mingled with a veneration for things old and beautiful from age that we love our old vices infinitely better than our new virtues." The English hate both evil and change.

"Hating the evil, we make the change, but we make it as small as possible." It seems natural, then, that *The Warden* should attack two "opposite evils." Trollope's double commitment does not show "an absence of all art-judgement in such matters." Rather, it permits him to express both sides of himself. Archdeacon Grantly and the young reformer, John Bold, embody the contradictory instincts of an author who paradoxically declared himself an "advanced conservative Liberal." Grantly represents Trollope's love of tradition and his loyalty to its institutions, while Bold speaks for his critical impulse and his zeal for reform. They are two sides of the civil servant who loved to obey orders promptly, while carefully explaining how fatuous the orders were. The inevitable result is a novel of dialectic, whose overall pattern is the synthesis or reconciliation of opposites. Thus the antithesis of Bold and Grantly is resolved in the warden, who represents a still deeper aspect of his maker's character: the tenderness, the need of affection, the shyness and melancholy which Trollope's bearish manner and aggressive practicality concealed. But besides the "realistic" characters and settings of Victorian social fiction, Trollope states his theme through a variety of techniques ranging from the personal allusions, parodies, and mock-heroic of Augustan satire to the symbols, allegories, and myths so dear to contemporary novelists. Thus he finds a precise symbolic notation for his pattern of conflict and reconciliation in the pervasive imagery of music. Our strategy will be to pursue this dialectic pattern, first in the characters and settings (as in Dickens, setting is a projection of character and vice versa), then in its ramifications of symbol and metaphor.

I

The conflict of Dr. Grantly and John Bold is more than a personal clash: it is the conflict of the Reformer with the Institution. A parson, writes Trollope in *Clergymen of the Church of England*, is so called because the parish clergyman is "the palpable and visible personage of the church in his parish, making that by his presence an intelligible reality, which, without, would be but an invisible idea." Archdeacon Grantly is clearly the "palpable and visible personage of the church" in the diocese of Barchester, and thus, for the purposes of the novel, an invisible idea is made an intelligible reality. Trollope stresses the point in a detailed mock-allegory of Dr. Grantly as a "fitting impersonation of a church militant." And a militant church it is. The archdeacon views it as a business and a stronghold, for in the competitive and acquisitive society of nineteenth-century England, it must wage a "never-ending battle" in defense of its revenues. Military and financial imagery permeate the book, reducing the traditional symbolism of Christian warfare to a squabble over shillings and pence, suggesting a world where money is, at least metaphorically, the measure of all things. When all values can be translated into economic terms, it is easy for the Church to confuse its revenues with " 'that better treasure to which thieves do not creep in.' " The archdeacon sees no distinction. "He did not believe in the Gospel with more assurance than he did in the sacred justice of all ecclesiastical revenues." Dr. Grantly is a penetrating study of the Official Mind, and for such a mind, the essential holiness of the Church extends to every aspect of its institutional life—including income.

This failure to distinguish inner meaning from outer forms produces the insistence on externals which marks all institutional thinking. We note Trollope's emphasis on the archdeacon's clerical uniform, from the "ever-new shovel hat" down to the black gaiters which reveal his well-turned leg, betokening "the outward beauty and grace of our church establishment." The sanctity of church dignitaries seems almost to reside in such outward graces: "Their clean and sombre apparel exacts from us faith and submission, and the cardinal virtues seem to hover round their sacred hats." But does the outer show belie the inner man? How does a bishop look without his apron, or an archdeacon in even a "lower state of dishabille"? Our curiosity is satisfied by the spectacle of Dr. Grantly nightcapped in the privacy of his bedroom. This "sainted enclosure" is but one of the many we are privileged to enter: the archdeacon's study with its secret drawer, the seclusion of the warden's garden and the privacy of his quad, the hallowed quiet of the cathedral "close." It is part of the charm of *The Warden* that it admits us to the security and order of a sheltered world. But there is the further, special lure of the institutional novel, the chance to get behind the façade of the Establishment, to glimpse its workings—and workers—from the inside. Seen out of uniform, in his bedroom, the archdeacon seems a different, even an "ordinary" man. And yet even in bed, he remains "archdeacon" to his wife.

The rest of the Plumstead rectory exhibits the same contrast of outer show and inner truth and the same bland diffusion of institutional tone. (The pleasing connotations of fruit and orchards which "Plumstead" evokes are misleading. The ecclesiastical "plum" is intended. In *Clergymen of the Church of England*, Trollope condemns the nepotism by which so many archdeacons were the sons of bishops.) Its "thorough clerical aspect" extends even to furniture, drapes and tableware. As the warden's "sacred music" suggests a religion of taste and feeling which is almost an aesthetic, so the thickness and heaviness of the Plumstead furniture, the solidity of the Plumstead tea service betoken a practical and mundane religion of cost and use. The archdeacon's study gives us the best image of his mind. About the edges of the room are bookshelves "loaded with theology." But the actual furnishings seem calculated for comfort and diversion, and locked up, presumably somewhere near the center of the room, is the archdeacon's copy of Rabelais. The psychological implications are clear enough. The archdeacon, "stretching out vastly his huge arms and opening his burly chest," himself suggests a Rabelaisian giant, but the gargantuan appetites implied by the cornucopia of the Plumstead breakfast table have been locked up and hidden away in the interests of clerical propriety. The result is a way of life neither exuberant nor spiritual. The colors in the rectory are somber, its heavy furnishings seem curiously lifeless, and "excellent as were the viands and the wines . . . I generally found the rectory somewhat dull." The archdeacon's profession has sublimated all his energies into an appetite for "church dominion," a love of power reflected in his wife and the political maneuverings of his sons.

In *Clergymen of the Church of England*, Trollope speaks of the parson's almost necessary hypocrisy. He is "compelled to have an inner life and an outer." Hence, "a parish parson among his own friends differs much from the parish parson among his parishioners." If Dr. Grantly realizes that he behaves differently at family prayers and in private with his wife, in his wife's company and alone in his study, these discrepancies do not trouble him. He senses no incongruity about that "inner room" where he keeps both "boots and sermons," and he unhesitatingly reveals his hidden Rabelais to the diocesan steward, a man "initiated into the comfortable arcana of ecclesiastical snuggeries." The insensitivity of the official conscience saves Dr. Grantly from real dishonesty. Indeed, despite his necessary hypocrisy, Trollope regards the parson as "a man always on the alert to be honest." The archdeacon sincerely serves the Church according to his lights. A window of his study looks toward the parish church; the two are linked by a "broad green path" and by the single paragraph in which both are described. The archdeacon's character is imaged in the church as well as the study: the body is too low and the tower too lofty, but the whole impresses us as strong and solid. Though the church does not quite reproduce the cross which is its pattern, its tone is richly indigenous, and it is full of characteristic and beautiful detail. We pass the same judgment on the building and the man: "Though in gazing on such a structure one knows by rule that the old priests who built it, built it wrong, one cannot bring oneself to wish that they should have made it other than it is."

Trollope conceived Dr. Grantly as a dignitary rather than an individual: "It was such as that, in my opinion, that an archdeacon should be." So too he sometimes calls Bold simply "the reformer." It is therefore significant that Bold's fortune goes back only one generation, that his father was not a native of Barchester, that his home is never described. His income derives from shops, an inn, and "the new row of genteel villas (so called in the advertisements), built outside the town beyond Hiram's Hospital." This environment of new money and so-called gentility is the proper setting for a "reformer"—just *outside* the town. In this enclosed society, the reformer is distinctly an outsider, with no deep roots in native soil, no well-defined place in the cathedral community. For unlike his counterparts at Rochester and St. Cross, Bold is not a clergyman. Since the reformer undertakes to cure abuses—a metaphor explicit in the parody of Carlyle—he becomes a doctor. But not a general practitioner like Dr. Thorne, who, in a later novel, acts as healer of a sick society: Bold's vocation of surgeon implies a more drastic, painful, and destructive therapy. And with no financial need to bind bruises and set limbs, all the brusque energy suggested in his name goes to "mend mankind." His brashness and dogmatism are those of youth confronted by tradition and convention: in a novel about the middle-aged and elderly, he is emphatically young. His radicalism, product of this youthful energy, is as instinctive as the archdeacon's conservatism—the drives of id and ego are concealed equally by high principles or high church. And as the archdeacon's appetite for life is channeled into a love of power, so Bold's "passion" for reform is easily diverted into love for Mr. Harding's daughter Eleanor.

Trollope shows how easily the idealist is exploited by others who invoke his principles. In attacking the Church, Bold becomes a tool of the Press: lacking a defined place in Barchester, he is drawn into the ambience of London and falls under the influence of Tom Towers, editor of the *Jupiter*. The symbolic opposition of Barchester and London, the cathedral city and the national capital, is deliberate and obvious: it is the old antithesis of the Church and the World. The *Jupiter*, that great London daily, directly competes with the Church as a source of moral authority. It is represented as a rival church with its own pope and inquisition, its vatican, issuing " 'infallible bulls for the guidance of British souls and bodies.' " Its holy spirit is the *Zeitgeist*; it speaks for the secular conscience of its time and place: "Such is Mount Olympus, the mouthpiece of all the wisdom of this great country. It may probably be said that no place in this 19th century is more worthy of notice." Hence the allusions to pagan religion which Trollope scatters with a free (and heavy) hand. Though Mount Olympus is the abode of gods and (presumably printer's) devils, its presiding deity is found—aptly enough—in the Temple. Here, proclaimed in mock-heroics, is the very shrine of the religion of justice, "the most favoured abode of Themis." And here, partaking nectar and ambrosia in the shape of toast and tea, we encounter a euhemeristic version of Mr. Anticant's godly man. For despite his human appearance, Tom Towers knows within his breast he is a god.

Bold finds both Dr. Grantly and Tom Towers in their studies, and by detailed contrasts and parallels between the rooms and men, Trollope hints that the editor is both the opposite and counterpart of the clergyman. Among these contrasts, we notice that instead of a window opening on the church, Towers's study boasts a painting of a "female devotee" by Millais. Again we detect the theme of past and present, for Trollope indicates that the Pre-Raphaelites have copied the mannerisms of mediaeval art while spoiling its meaning. Instead of traditional subjects, the love, the ecstasy and endurance of the saints, they offer "pain without grace and abstraction without a cause." They substitute the religion of beauty for the beauty of religion: the "devotee" pays her devotions to a lily. And this religion is divorced from life—framed, glazed, set upon a pedestal. The devotional lady, "drawn in a position which it is impossible to suppose any figure should maintain," is easily translated into a comment on the lofty ecclesiastical ideals of the *Jupiter*. But we notice parallels with Dr. Grantly, too. The archdeacon's legal strategy, which the *Jupiter* denounces as "peculiarly revolting to the minds of English churchmen," is precisely the strategy Towers now uses against Bold. Both avoid fixing awkward responsibilities through an institutional anonymity: the warden serves unnamed employees; the *Jupiter*'s editorials are by an unknown hand. Churchman and journalist, the servants of truth, both reject truths which do not fit their views; both represent institutions which they defend against outside "interference," but which they themselves exploit in their common love of power. And these are the institutions which contend for influence over the English mind and conscience. Clearly we have reached a moral stalemate. In the hands of the churchman and the editor, a problem of justice has dwindled to a legal quibble, a conflict of ideas to a gambit in institutional power politics. And likewise between the archdeacon and the reformer there seems no possible ground of reconciliation. It is to the warden we must turn.

II

The warden is well suited to his role of mediator. Like the archdeacon, he is a clergyman and a firm pillar of the establishment, but like Bold, he is a reformer. He has "greatly improved" the Barchester choir—though he sees still further "room for improvement"—and he is sharply critical of morning service in Westminster Abbey. But unlike Bold, he recognizes the "impropriety" of "meddling" in Abbey affairs. And he naturally turns to "our ancient church music" for his new anthology, *Harding's Church Music*. He is committed to both past and present, institution and reform. He differs from the archdeacon on the nature of the institution, however, and from Bold on the motives for reform. These differences we must explore to understand the warden's central position in the novel.

In essence, Harding is a man of feeling and Bold a man of principle. The reformer thinks and talks in impersonal categories and abstractions: justice, right and wrong, the public interest. He deals with the bedesmen of the Hospital through his lawyer, Finney. For Bold, "these poor men" stand collectively for "the poor of the city of Barchester generally." But for Mr. Harding, the bedesmen are "old neighbours" whom he knows and loves by name. He cares little for public interests though he dreads the loss of "public sympathy."

The logic of principle is clear. "What is unjust must be wrong," reasons Bold; "what is wrong should be righted." But Mr. Harding seems to feel his way intuitively to decisions. The possibility that "the young man is right and that I am wrong" is less a clear and distinct idea than an uneasiness which gradually deepens to acute unhappiness. The constant recurrence of "happy" and "unhappy" marks the primitive antithesis of pleasure and pain on which Trollope's ethics and psychology depend. His moral hedonism assumes that we must be satisfied with ourselves in order to be happy. The "Barchester Brutus" in the "self-devotion" of his "singular virtue" can comfort himself for the loss of Eleanor Harding with meditation on his own stoic heroism. Because Dr. Grantly is so satisfied with himself and his order, he is easily satisfied by the attorney-general's legal quibbles. But Mr. Harding is not "self-satisfied of the justice of his own cause," so the archdeacon's arguments fail to satisfy him. (See chapter 9, where "satisfy" and its cognates occur thirteen times in almost the same number of pages.) Tormented by a moral sensitivity which has no argument but suffering, the warden is indeed hard to satisfy. But in the happy world of Barchester, it is precisely this capacity for suffering which marks him as a hero.

Bold draws clear antitheses between principle and feeling, public good and private motives, suppressing love for Eleanor and friendship for her father in the name of duty. Conduct impelled by feeling lacks this logical rigor, for it reflects the ambiguities of its source. Setting out to do what he feels to be right, Mr. Harding experiences the sensations of an escaped convict or truant schoolboy. He is both hero and coward, and his moral strength begins in weakness: he cannot bear to be misjudged and first conceives his resignation as an escape from an uncomfortable position. The complexities of feeling are easily misinterpreted. In chapter 6, their mutual concern leads the warden and his daughter to misunderstand each other's motives. But soon Mr. Harding is explaining his own ambiguous position and sympathizing with Eleanor's divided heart. Bold's position is much simpler, yet in the same chapter, he fails in explaining it to his sister: "Why it's a long story, and I don't know that I can make you understand it." For all their complex feelings, father and daughter understand one another; for all his logic and his principles, brother and sister do not.

In the latter half of the book, both men realize they have been wrong. (If we treat the last chapter as a coda, the action covers twenty chapters. In the first ten, Bold triumphs and the warden suffers; in the last ten, Bold suffers and the warden triumphs. The second half divides into two units of five chapters, the first mainly devoted to Bold's actions, the second to the warden's. Chapter 13, "The Warden's Decision," serves to undercut Bold's self-sacrifice by showing its futility and prevents the analogies of chapters 12 and 14 from seeming repetitious.) Paradoxically, Bold is converted by an appeal to feeling, while Mr. Harding decides by principle. The reformer, who opposed principles to feelings, simply reverses his field. Actuated now by love of Eleanor, he must experience the ambiguities and misinterpretations that attend such impulses. Even the exultation of a happy lover is "not without a shade of remorse." The archdeacon misjudges his motives and "outrages" his feelings; Tom Towers turns against him his own cant of public virtue and private interests. Bold has learned to distrust such abstract simplifications. A public issue is a conglomeration of private interests, not a collision of right and wrong, and "it takes an age to ascertain the truth of any question." But Bold has contradicted himself in "giving up the resolve of many hours of thought to the tears of a pretty girl," and his inconsistency is punished in his humiliating meetings with the journalist and the archdeacon.

The warden's contrasting interviews with Sir Abraham Haphazard and Dr. Grantly seem positively triumphant. His sensibility admits no division between feeling and principle, private motives and public duty. In resigning, he does what he has long desired, but does it now because it is right. The evolution through uneasiness and mental anguish to moral recognition is slow, but it is an evolution and not a reversal. The whole weight of the warden's character is behind his final declaration that the *Jupiter*'s arguments represent "truth," that he has no "right" to his position. But though this decision has become for him a matter of principle, he claims for it only the validity of a personal feeling: " 'A man is the best judge of what he feels himself.' " His solution, based on "an inward and unguided conviction of my own," applies only to himself. He can thus side with the reformers without casting a "slur" on the institution: "My resignation of the wardenship need offer not the slightest bar to its occupation by another person." But this example of self-sacrifice inspires his daughter to play Iphigenia and ultimately reconciles the opposed forces. The "public question" becomes personal. Bold confesses himself in the wrong—because Mr. Harding's conduct has been " 'so excellent, so little selfish, so open.' "

The bishop tacitly confesses the need for reform, refusing to appoint another warden—it would be wrong to make him suffer as Mr. Harding has. There is no need of courts of law; the case has been decided in the "court" of one man's conscience, and the contending parties accept a "judgement without power of appeal."

Thus Mr. Harding proves a more effective reformer than John Bold. He is also a more effective churchman than Dr. Grantly. Gradually he replaces the archdeacon as true representative of the Church: by the end of the book, Dr. Grantly represents the "spiritualities of the diocese of Barchester" only in the eyes of Messrs. Cox and Cumming. Both clergymen differ essentially from a secular thinker like John Bold. The reformer invokes an ideal abstraction, a " 'dream of justice' " to which human actions and institutions must conform. The churchman's faith is in an incarnation: his ideals are concretely manifested in the Church and in its founder. But Harding and Grantly differ on the nature of this embodiment. The archdeacon's church is an institution; the warden's, a community.

The warden's conception prevails, for only in a community bound by mutual sympathy could his example have effect. And it is life in such a community which has fostered Mr. Harding's special moral sensibility. If the characters of Bold and Grantly are determined by the theme of the book, Mr. Harding is the distillation of its atmosphere. Barchester is essentially a state of mind, a way of life. Reiterated words like ease, kindly, quiet, pleasant establish its peculiar tone. But above all, life in the Barchester close means "comfort"—a word which, with its cognates, is repeated at least fifty times. As its name suggests, the "close" is a secluded precinct, a nook or corner which is warm and snug as well as quiet, decent, and sweet. Add to these the more dignified terms Trollope also uses for his ecclesiastical settings—beauty, antiquity, order—and we have the diction of a golden world. The focus of this diction is "our good, kind, loving warden": these values, this character are the human equivalents of the cathedral setting.

As the archdeacon's view of the Church is reflected in Plumstead, so the warden's is reflected in his Hospital. It is a community literally and figuratively founded upon charity. Nevertheless it is a class society: a "slight iron screen" separates the bedesmen's dwellings from Mr. Harding's. Trollope trusts "feeling," but he distinguishes the feelings of a pauper and a gentleman. Both aim at happiness, but while Eleanor could be happy with only bread to eat, the bedesmen want one hundred pounds a year. But the Hospital does show that "tendency towards equality" which was Trollope's social ideal: Mr. Bunce passes the slight iron barrier to take wine in Mr. Harding's parlor. We note that in the Hospital, unlike the diocese, the aggressive administrative tendencies of Bunce and Grantly are subordinate to more sympathetic and unworldly tendencies represented by the warden and the bishop.

Seen through the gateway that divides it from the dust and traffic of the London road, the Hospital with its river, its well-mown lawn and noble trees looks very like a paradise. But when we enter the warden's garden, its communal harmony is already threatened. The snake-like Finney also finds his way in, "asking sly questions, and raising immoderate hopes." The warden himself passes from innocence to knowledge of his own involvement in guilt. He must abandon his "Elysium," and at the end of the book, Mr. Harding and Eleanor pass arm in arm into the world. The lost paradise becomes a "wretched wilderness": "The beauty of the place is gone."

Though the idyllic society of the Hospital is thus destroyed, the sympathy of father and daughter creates a perfect community in miniature. The scenes between them, so sentimental to us, are essential to the theme. Her father's suffering inspires Eleanor to sacrifice herself; his daughter's approval sustains Mr. Harding in his resolution. Paradoxically, this community of feeling admits conflict of interests. The warden actually encourages his daughter's love for his opponent, while she urges her father to resign the income which ensures her future. True to his isolating ideals, Bold feels that he must decline the warden's invitations. But eventually the sympathy of father and daughter draws both official and reformer within its field. John Bold and Dr. Grantly are never reconciled on principles, but through their relations to Eleanor and Mr. Harding they become "almost friends." Thus concord is restored in a community where virtually all the major characters are united in a single family.

III

To understand the full significance of Mr. Harding's lonely, gentle heroism, we need to recognize in Hiram's Hospital something resembling allegory. Trollope, who imitates so many devices of

Augustan satire and freely plagiarizes *The Rape of the Lock,* may well have copied John Hiram's will from *A Tale of a Tub.* There the history of the Church is allegorized through the changing interpretations placed upon a will (with an obvious pun on "testament"). Trollope's Hospital is not a symbol of the Church, nor is John Hiram a type of its founder. But Trollope helps us see analogies between the problems which confront both institutions. Like the Hospital, the Church is an institution founded on charity and theoretically united in love. Both were established in the remote past by "godly" men whose enigmatic intentions can be interpreted only through their written testaments and their own "godlike work." Both institutions have passed through "bad times" to prosperity; both must now interpret the literal terms of the "testament" to fit new social conditions, while remaining true to the original "will" of the founder. Gradually, as differing interpretations are put forward, we realize the difficulty of deciding precisely what John Hiram meant or how his meaning can be adopted to circumstances he did not foresee. (John Bold, with the simplicity of the secular mind, is sure that the Church is perverting the obvious meaning of the will. The old bishop cannot refute the charge: he has not read the will since he was instituted—if then! But the archdeacon, who has " 'got up all that,' " maintains the claim of a learned church to interpret its own documents. His interpretation is dogmatic. " 'You have not read John Hiram's will,' " he tells the bedesmen. " '. . . I have; I know what his will was; and I tell you that that was his will, and that was his intention.' ") How, then, shall his will be done? It is this question the warden answers by his conduct.

The answer is not so much what he does as how and why he does it. Indeed, the real action of the novel is psychological. Already in the second chapter Mrs. Grantly foresees that Bold's marriage will end his meddling, and in the very first chapter, we learn that the warden has tried to silence criticism by surrendering part of his income, "feeling that there might be truth in what had been said"— has succeeded, moreover, by announcing his intent before the archdeacon could intervene. Thus the resolution of both plots is foreshadowed from the start. The real interest lies in the development of attitude and motive, the warden's growth from weakling to hero as the action he contemplates evolves from unmanly evasion to a bitterly regretted duty and finally to a willed and perfect sacrifice. It is this perfecting of the will which makes an action holy, which constitutes a sacrifice in the root sense of that word. The archetypal sacrifice was offered with the words "thy will be done" (Matt. 26:42), words echoed by the warden in another garden: " '—God's will be done.' " The echo suggests the meaning of his action. He resolves conflict in the main plot by giving up his position, and in the subplot by giving up his daughter; he leaves his garden and his home; in a real sense he gives up his life. Mr. Anticant's sarcastic analogy between the godly man of today and the godly man of long ago is fulfilled. We notice other such historic prototypes in the Barchester Brutus, in Eleanor's role as Iphigenia, in church dignitaries as "personifications of St. Paul." The contrast of these burlesque personifications prepares us to recognize in the warden's self-devotion as he sets his face towards London, a likeness to a higher model. Again we must avoid the temptations of allegory. Mr. Harding is no "Christ figure." An allegory or type of Christ points beyond itself, giving us through its figures a fresh understanding of the familiar biblical events. But the analogies which hover about the warden point only to him, helping to define and deepen the meaning of his sufferings for Trollope's fiction. These likenesses are suggestive, not systematic, and they are neither daring nor blasphemous. Every deeply Christian act involves this likeness; indeed, what precept is more familiar than the imitation of Christ?

That extraordinary chapter, "A Long Day in London," records Mr. Harding's Gethsemane. Isolated by his own foreknowledge and resolve, the warden takes "sanctuary" in the Abbey. There in solitude he can say his prayers and "think gravely of the step he was about to take." The humiliations and misery of the London eating house, with its "horrid mixture procured from the neighbouring public-house," is a foretaste of the cup of poverty which he now sees at his lips. But new strength comes to him in the "paradise" of the coffee divan with its civil old waiter and its musical clock; he is ready for what faces him and "absolutely enjoying himself." Nevertheless, the ordeal has been genuine, and so are the two trials which ensue. For the hero who obeys his private moral vision comes under judgment of the law, whether the authorities are Roman Governor and Jewish high priest or an English attorney-general and archdeacon. These represent the conventional codes of Church and State; the warden asserts his allegiance to a higher law. Leaving Sir Abraham (whose name may be significant), he finds "a calm, bright, beautiful night, and by the light of the moon, even the chapel of Lincoln's Inn, and the sombre row of chambers, which surround the quadrangle, looked well." The stronghold of legalism is momentarily transfigured; the warden seems almost to have redeemed a world which rejects him. Certainly he is himself transfigured. As he offers wine to his twelve bedesmen and bids them farewell, the eucharistic overtones seem unmistakable (there were thirteen paupers at St. Cross, but Trollope has altered the number). At the end of the book, he has literally ascended to a tiny church over the gateway to the close, where he still performs afternoon services and administers the Sacrament. It is, Trollope tell us, a "perfect church."

Thus Mr. Harding completes his "godlike work." This work is dual, for his position as both warden and precentor reflects the commitment of the Church to active charity and to devotion. Trollope was alert to the significance of ecclesiastical titles: in *Clergymen of the Church of England* he distinguishes carefully between "rector," "vicar," and "parson," and explains "incumbent" by reference to Johnson's *Dictionary*. Hence it seems probable that in changing the title of the Master of St. Cross, he knew that a warden is, by definition and etymology, a guardian. In fact, he refers to the two "guardians" of the Hospital, and allows the *Jupiter* a sneer at the "so-called warden." The archdeacon too considers himself a guardian: in preserving the Church's revenues, he is guarding its "citadel," defending the "holy of holies," fighting "the best of fights" to secure the "comforts of his creed" for future dignitaries like himself. The warden rebukes this materialism in the imagery of Christ: "Consider the ravens: for they neither sow nor reap; which neither have storehouse nor barn; and God feedeth them: how much more are ye better than the fowls" (Luke 12:24). Mr. Harding's appeal to "God that feeds the young ravens" reminds us through its biblical context that a man's life consists not in the abundance of things which he has, that he who lays up treasure for himself is not rich toward God (Luke 12:15, 21). The values which the warden guards are intangible, and the " 'better treasure' " to which Mr. Anticant refers can sometimes only be secured by surrendering that other wealth which the archdeacon considers sacred. In significant juxtaposition, the warden is said to be laying aside the title of his office just as the archdeacon takes up the outward signs of his: the "shining new clerical hat," the "black new clerical gloves." By resigning his title to the "comforts of his creed," Mr. Harding proves himself the true warden of its "spiritualities."

In the end, he is " 'not warden now, only precentor.' " The word which thus concludes the novel and was originally its title means, according to Dr. Johnson, "he that leads the choir." In his discussion of "incumbent," Trollope cites not only Johnson's definition, but also the illustrative quotation from Swift. If he looked up "precentor" in the *Dictionary,* it seems likely that he also noted the illustration from Henry Hammond's *Practical Catechism* (1644). Hammond explains that part of Christ's function as a priest after the order of Melchizedek is praising God forever in heaven. It is our duty to "follow this *precentor* of ours in blessing and magnifying that God of all grace, and never yielding to those enemies which he died to give us power to resist and overcome." To this priesthood of continual praise Mr. Harding is called in St. Cuthbert's over the close. Thus Trollope resolves the problems of continuity and human error suggested by the parodies of Dickens and Carlyle. Even in a "perfect church" human nature is not transformed. Only John Bold (or Mr. Popular Sentiment) could mistake Dr. Grantly for "a real devil here on earth," and even Eleanor Bold is only a "mortal angel." But the "perfect church" is founded on such mixed humanity: the supports of its "high pitched" roof terminate in grotesque faces, "two devils and an angel on one side, two angels and a devil on the other." Mr. Harding, more angel than devil to begin with, proves that ordinary humanity is capable of transfiguring heroism when it follows this precentor of ours, that a "godly man of latter days" may become genuinely Christ-like, and that thus the life of Christ in his Church is not merely continued but renewed.

IV

The precentor's music expresses "a soul alive to harmony." Moral conflict in Mr. Harding is akin to musical improvisation: in conversational perplexities, the passes on his imaginary cello are short and slow, the instrument concealed beneath his chair; "but as his spirit warmed to the subject—as his trusting heart, looking to the bottom of that which vexed him, would see its clear way out,—he would rise to a higher melody, sweep the unseen strings with a bolder hand, and swiftly fingering the cords . . . create an ecstatic strain of perfect music, audible to himself and to St. Cecilia, and not without effect." Thus Trollope uses what could have been simply an endearing oddity to strike the keynote of his novel. For *The Warden* exemplifies that theme of harmony which Leo Spitzer hears echoing so widely through Western literature, and the essential pattern of the book is the *concordia discors.*

We first hear music when, with John Bold, we come upon Mr. Harding playing to his bedesmen. Though the old men may not appreciate the concert, they try to give him pleasure by pretending to. Mr. Harding is plainly delighted to have an audience, but his delight springs from their admiration of the music, not of his performance. There is a touch of comic misunderstanding, and because the motives are not sentimentalized, we accept the idyllic image of a harmonious society. Even Bold is subdued by "such sweet harmony" to hesitate in introducing a "theme of so much discord," and the garden seems in truth "a precinct specially fit for the worship of St. Cecilia." But there are other hints of discord: two bedesmen no longer find Mr. Harding's music to their taste, while Bunce, who seems to think both music and musician "heavenly," perhaps is but a flatterer.

A harmony founded on such an unreal community of interest cannot last: the golden world is evoked only to be disrupted. Its diction of ease and happiness is replaced by that of a fallen world: anxious, painful, cruel, miserable. "Comfort" still recurs, but its meaning changes from pleasure to consolation. Meanwhile, a murmur of scandal has become a crisis of conscience for the entire community, and what seemed a simple problem grows increasingly complex as the archdeacon and the *Jupiter,* John Bold and Mr. Bunce present their differing views. The progress of the argument is dialectical, and Trollope argues all sides persuasively. The archdeacon's speech on loyalty is splendidly phrased and strongly reasoned; the *Jupiter's* editorials are unfair but unanswerable. The contending interests are played off against each other in vigorous counterpoint; the theme is doubled, inverted, transposed till all its complexities are before us. We are reminded that justice is not law, that even perfect justice may not make the bedesmen and the warden happier, that the economics of happiness differ for a pauper and a gentleman. We realize that we were lulled by the specious calm of the first chapter, that its serenity concealed ironies and covert tensions: Mr. Harding's "munificence" of tuppence a day, the slightly lavish insistence on Mr. Chadwick's "worthiness," the hints of nepotism, the indication that Mr. Harding is "never quite at ease in money matters." The bland assertion that Mr. Harding holds "one of the most coveted of

. . . snug clerical sinecures" at first seems only cause to congratulate the "happy warden." By the time we hear of Crabtree Canonicorum and Dr. Vesey Stanhope, we know that a "very nice thing" means a monstrous abuse, and the connotations of force-feeding and sloth in "Goosegorge" and "Eiderdown" hardly seem exaggerated. Yet the neighboring parish of Crabtree with its poor curate is Mr. Harding's: he too is a nonresident pluralist. It is this underlying moral stringency which saves Trollope's world from oversweetness, and yet the morality is never harsh because it is never simple-minded. We are compelled to a view at once more tolerant and more sharp, but with our sense of increased moral precision comes a sense of increased practical difficulty. The problem of John Hiram's will seems insoluble—indeed, it remains unsolved at the end of the book. Only Mr. Harding, looking to the bottom of these perplexities, sees his "clear way out."

As precentor, he leads the music in which the counterpoint of contending interests is finally resolved. Gradually, in spite of wasted energy and personal suffering, a "higher melody" emerges. If the warden's paradise is lost, the womblike innocence of the close had become a prison to escape, as Dr. Grantly's pedagogy is a school he has outgrown. The old man whom the archdeacon still treats as a child has suddenly matured. He has confronted the moral perplexity of the adult world, advancing, in the words of Mr. Anticant, to an " 'infinite state of freedom and knowledge of good and evil,' " and has regained, through doubt and anguish, what Michael promised Adam, the happier Paradise within. This sequence of false harmony giving way to discord and resolved in truer harmony underlies the musical shaping of the book. It is repeated in smaller units, like the sequence of the Abbey, the supper house, and the coffee divan in "A Long Day in London." But the paradigm is clearest in the chapter which balances "A Long Day" in the first half of the book, "The Warden's Tea Party." Once more the association of music and community is stressed: the false concord of good manners, with its stiff discomfort and embarrassed distances, gives way to the cheerful melee of a happy party, and the catalyst is music. Encouraged by these "sweeter sounds," gamblers and lovers begin their little games. Both whist and flirtation are described as combats: beaux and belles exchange blows "fatal, incurable, dealing death"; the poor archdeacon is "speechless in his agony." Even the music echoes these struggles, "now loud, as though stirring the battle, then low as though mourning the slain." But the mock-heroic, by a typical inversion, suggests that the financial contest of the main plot may be no more disastrous than a game of cards, that the estrangement of the sweethearts in the subplot is but another strategy in the wars of love. Even the sufferings of Mr. Harding, poured out in the "touching tale" of that "saddest of instruments," his cello, are but excursions in a minor key before the lively coda. Agony like that of the archdeacon, the lovers, or even Mr. Harding, is preliminary to a keener pleasure, and the cello instructs us that there must be tension and discord before the "sweeter sounds" begin: "How often were those pegs twisted and re-twisted before our friend found that he had twisted them enough; how many discordant scrapes gave promise of the coming harmony!"

This reconciliation of pleasure and pain is only one example of *concordia discors*. Past and present, human and divine, feeling and principle, the reformer and the institution, the outsider and the community, the Church and the World—all the antinomies which we have traced are harmonized. The reformer is needed to challenge the complacency of institutions; the community assimilates the insight of outsiders; the secular conscience compels the Church to revive its past, making what is human in its nature resemble more what is divine. Nevertheless, the novel finally justifies the institutional religion of the Church. Its misuse of worldly goods is far less vicious than the World's misuse of religion: witness Sir Abraham and the "Convent Custody Bill." It is within the Christian community that interests conflict without impairing sympathy, that a conglomeration of private interests can work in musical counterpoint so that even the discords of self-righteousness and bigotry give promise of a harmony to come. And it is from inside that the Church is effectually reformed. The purest and most complex moral consciousness which we encounter is Mr. Harding's, and his sensibility, for which principle has the immediacy of feeling, is shaped by a life of devotion in a community of love. That is the claim of the Church in a utilitarian age.

The Church, then, is not the rotten building derided by Tom Towers, nor even the aging structure which the archdeacon keeps in such good repair. It is a living thing, a community, but its life depends on the vitality of the solitary conscience. Through sympathy, the community responds to the "dream of justice" of its heroes. But the revolution of feeling is slow; meanwhile it exacts suffering of the one who would redeem it: " 'It is he that has to bear the punishment, it is he that suffers.' " In the midst of the party comes a melancholy solo: "Now alone that saddest of instruments tells its touching tale. Silent, and in awe, stand fiddle, flute, and piano, to hear the sorrows of their wailing brother." And at the center of the book, in the chapter entitled "Tribulation," even this is silenced. "He could never again lift up his voice boldly as he had hitherto done among his brethren, for he felt that he was disgraced; and he feared even to touch his bow, for he knew how grievous a sound of wailing, how piteous a lamentation it would produce." There is a place, then, in the novel's music for the clamors of battle and the lamentation of grief. But the total pattern intimates that even conflict and suffering are elements of some larger music, audible to a "soul alive to harmony." It is a strain of that "perfect music" which Mr. Harding captures when, seeing his clear way at last, he strikes up "such a tune as never before had graced the chambers of any attorney-general. He was standing up, gallantly fronting Sir Abraham, and his right arm passed with bold and rapid sweeps before him, as though he were embracing some huge instrument, which allowed him to stand thus erect; and with the fingers of his left hand he stopped, with preternatural velocity, a multitude of strings."

One wonders about the huge instrument which thus supports the warden. One pictures the cross formed by the bow upon the strings; one recalls Auden's image of the great cellist "crucified over his instrument." But surely this is going too far. Already I have been far too explicit concerning matters which are felt in reading as resonances and reverberations, as echoes and overtones in a novel which, among the English novels of its day, approaches most nearly the condition of music.

*T*he *Warden:* Novel of Vocation

Hugh L. Hennedy

Although Henry James imagined Trollope as saying, "Judge me in the lump. . . ; I have only undertaken to entertain the British public. I don't pretend that each of my novels is an organic whole," he did think that *The Warden* had "a certain classic roundness, though . . . there is a blemish on its fair face." The "blemish," James thought, was chapter 15, which satirizes Carlyle and Dickens through the figures of Dr. Pessimist Anticant and Mr. Popular Sentiment. James regarded that chapter as "a mistake almost inconceivable," and the parodies of Carlyle and Dickens "as infelicitous as they are misplaced." James also thought that "it was no less luckless an inspiration to convert Archdeacon Grantley's [sic] three sons, denominated respectively Charles James, Henry and Samuel, into little effigies of three distinguished English bishops of that period, whose well-known peculiarities are reproduced in the description of these unnatural urchins. The whole passage, as we meet it, is a sudden disillusionment; we are transported from the mellow atmosphere of an assimilated Barchester to the air of ponderous allegory."

Until recently most critics have agreed with James about chapter 15, and even Michael Sadleir did not care to defend the novel against James's charge. Indeed, his own criticism of the offending chapter is at least as strong as James's, for he finds the parody and satire of the

---

From *Unity in Barsetshire.* © 1971 by Mouton & Co., N.V.

chapter "extraneous to the story's theme," "in direct conflict with the story's spirit," and "foreign to the story's very purpose."

Although in 1947 one critic (Lionel Stevenson) chose to defend the parody of Dickens on biographical-historical grounds, it was not until 1962 that anyone arose to defend the chapter on structural grounds. Sherman Hawkins, seeing the subject of *The Warden* as "the Church, and the paradoxes and problems which arise when an impulse of the spirit must be translated into a corporation with a bank account," argues that chapter 15 is structurally important, for "the parodies of Anticant and Sentiment suggest problems of continuity and human fallibility central, in any Protestant view, to institutional religion."

Hawkins's essay is so persuasive that one finishes it with a feeling that chapter 15 is an important chapter of an unusually well-constructed novel. Not only that, but the essay inclines one to agree with Hawkins's assertions that *The Warden* is not only "perhaps the most perfectly integrated of the Barchester novels," but also the "novel which, among the English novels of its day, approaches most nearly the condition of music." If one now persists in writing about *The Warden,* he does so not so much with the intention of refuting Hawkins as with that of supplementing him.

The Church is indeed one of the central subjects of *The Warden,* and Archdeacon Grantly is, as Hawkins says he is, "clearly the palpable and visible personage of the Church in the diocese of Barchester." But if Dr. Grantly, "the archdeacon militant," represents the Church as an institution, if Trollope portrays him as looking "like an ecclesiastical statue placed there, as a fitting impersonation of the church militant here on earth," Trollope also pictures him as a professional man: "His shovel hat, large, new, and well-pronounced, a churchman's hat in every inch, declared the profession as plainly as does the Quaker's broad brim." Trollope also sees the archdeacon as representing a "political" position, one abstracted from the Church or not necessarily connected with it: if Trollope sees Mr. Harding's "possible son-in-law, Bold," as "the reformer," he also sees the warden's "positive son-in-law," the archdeacon," as "the conservative." Furthermore, if Dr. Grantly is one of the novel's most important characters, he is no more important than John Bold, who does not represent the Church.

It appears, then, that though it is true to say that the archdeacon represents the visible Church, such a statement presents only part of the truth about the archdeacon. Similarly, to take the Church as the subject of *The Warden* is to narrow down the scope of the work, for as catholic as the Church may be, the subject of *The Warden* is broader. *The Warden* is not so much "about" an institution as institutions: it is concerned with the press, for instance, as well as the Church. Moreover, the book is less concerned with institutions than it is with those who run them. *The Warden*, in other words, is about vocations, and it is best seen as a prose *Lycidas*.

Hawkins has noted that *The Warden* not only "imitates . . . many devices of Augustan satire" but also "freely plagiarizes *The Rape of the Lock*." The card game of chapter 6, "The Warden's Tea Party," is probably the most obvious example of such "plagiarism." Hawkins also points out a number of parallels between *The Warden* and *Paradise Lost*: "Seen through the gateway that divides it from the dust and traffic of the London road, the Hospital with its river, its well-mown lawn and noble trees looks very like a paradise. . . . At the end of the book Mr. Harding and Eleanor pass arm and arm into the world." As real as these literary presences are in *The Warden,* that of Milton's earlier poem, *Lycidas*, a poem to which Trollope was passionately attached in his young manhood, is more significant, and the objections of those critics who, like James and Sadleir, have disliked the parodies of Carlyle and Dickens in *The Warden* make as much sense as objections to the "digressions" in *Lycidas,* for in both works the problem of vocation is uppermost, and *The Warden's* chapter 15 concerns itself with the vocations of priest, journalist, prophet, and novelist, as the "digressions" of the poem attack the problems of the vocations of poet and priest.

Of the two evils which Trollope, in the *Autobiography*, says he intended to attack in *The Warden*, the first, "the possession by the Church of certain funds and endowments which had been intended for charitable purposes, but which had been allowed to become income for idle Church dignitaries," might, simply as a subject, remind readers of Milton's attack on the idle shepherds. But as the novel develops and one hears a denunciation of "the grasping priests of the Church of England [who] are gorged with the wealth which the charity of former times has left for the solace of the aged, or the education of the young," one begins to hear the Miltonic tone. And later on when Gregory Moody, one of the more aggressive of Hiram's bedesmen, growls, one hears the very language of *Lycidas*: " 'Sink them all for parsons, say I,' growled Moody; 'hungry beggars, as never thinks their bellies full till they have robbed all and everything!' "

But if the novel echoes *Lycidas*, the similarities do not end there, for it has its pastoral, if not elegiac, elements, and they are important. John Hiram, the fifteenth-century endower of Hiram's Hospital, made his money as a woolstapler, and he willed that the hospital be established "for the support of twelve superannuated wool-carders." These vocations of woolstapling and wool-carding are the first mentioned in the novel, except for that of clergyman, Mr. Harding's calling. At the time of the action of the novel, however, there are no more wool-carders left in Barchester, "so the bishop, dean, and warden, who took it in turn to put in the old men, generally appointed some hangers-on of their own; worn-out gardeners, decrepit gravediggers, or octogenarian sextons." Here is the first instance in the novel of a deviation from the letter of Hiram's will, a document which, by the way, is not reproduced in the novel, so that its terms remain for the reader somewhat vague, a condition which Trollope probably intended as one means of emphasizing the complexity and difficulty of the moral issues raised in the novel. In any event, it is clear from the start that John Hiram made his money from sheep and that he intended his endowment to take care of men who had worked with sheep or sheep products. Trollope may even this early in the novel be foreshadowing its outcome, since if the men whom the will intended to benefit no longer exist, why is a warden needed for them?

If one does not at the beginning of the novel clearly see Mr. Harding, the warden, as a pastor, as a shepherd appointed to care for the carers of the sheep, the demise of wool-carding is an obvious reason for such vagueness of vision. It is worth noting, however, that at at least one point in the novel Trollope does image one of Mr. Harding's charges as a sheep. When Handy, Moody, and Spriggs try to pressure the three undecided bedesmen into signing the petition to the bishop, Billy Gazy, one of the undecided, is asked to think about their arguments. "But Billy Gazy couldn't think: he made a noise like the bleating of an old sheep, which was intended to express the agony of his doubt, and again muttered that 'he didn't know.' "

At the end of the novel, Billy Gazy, along with five other bedesmen, is dead. Mr. Harding having resigned and the bishop having refused to appoint a successor to him, the old men have had to face death without a warden to care for them. Mr. Harding, it is true, "did not desert them; from him they had such consolation as a dying man may receive from his Christian pastor; but it was the occasional kindness of a stranger which ministered to them, and not the constant presence of a master, a neighbour, and a friend." Though it is clear that the bedesmen have suffered without their warden, it is also apparent that Mr. Harding, without his wardenship, functions more distinctly as a Christian pastor, for the demise of wool-carding in Barchester is but one cause for Mr. Harding's not appearing clearly as a pastor at the beginning of the novel.

For one thing, Mr. Harding had come to Barchester originally not to fill the position of warden but, because of "a fine voice and a taste for sacred music," he had come to perform "the easy but not highly paid duties of a minor canon." When he was forty, Mr. Harding had been given the living of Crabtree Parva, and for ten years he had functioned actively as pastor of that small parish while still performing his canonical duties; but when, at fifty, he had been made precentor of the cathedral and warden of the hospital, he had handed over to a curate the duties and small income of Crabtree Parva. At the beginning of the novel, then, Mr. Harding is not functioning as the pastor of a parish, and though his position as warden has its pastoral elements, changing times and the demise of wool-carding have made that position highly ambiguous.

Since the shepherd of the pastoral tradition is a singer or poet as well as, sometimes, a priest, it is certainly worth noting that Mr. Harding's chief duty, both as canon and as precentor, is to sing. And although Dr. Anticant supposes that the modern counterpart of John Hiram, " 'the godly man of four centuries since,' " sings " 'indifferently through his nose once in the week some psalm more or less long—the shorter the better, we should be inclined to say,' " the truth is that the fine voice and the interest in sacred music which brought Mr. Harding to Barchester in the first place have never deserted him. Indeed, in this part of his vocation Mr. Harding is unexcelled. At the end of the novel, "Mr. Harding is still precentor of Barchester; and it is very rarely the case that those who attend the Sunday morning service miss the gratification of hearing him chant the Litany as no other man in England can do it." And under Mr. Harding's guidance, the Barchester choir has been so improved that it "now rivals that of any cathedral in England." Mr. Harding's chief avocations, playing the cello and publishing and writing about ancient church music also, of course, help to locate him within the pastoral convention of the shepherd-musician.

Mr. Harding's doubts about his right to the income from the wardenship begin fairly early in the novel—they begin almost immediately after John Bold's announcement in chapter 3 that he intends to look into the carrying-out of John Hiram's will—and they continue "for many a long, long day" until, in chapter 13, the warden decides to give up the wardenship. Mr. Harding is unsure of some of the consequences attendant upon his resignation and, while he is waiting to see Sir Abraham Haphazard, he spends some of his long day in London in Westminster Abbey trying to figure out how he can adjust the duties of Crabtree Parva with those of his precentorship. As it turns out, he does not have to turn his curate out of Crabtree Parva, but the point is that as many doubts as Mr. Harding may have during the course of the novel, of one thing he is sure: he wants to retain the precentorship. That position, he is sure, remains a central part of his calling as a clergyman.

Trollope's original title for his novel was *The Precentor*, but he was persuaded by his publishers to let it be published as *The Warden*. The original title emphasizes the certain, whereas the final title calls attention to the ambiguous, part of Mr. Harding's vocation. The first is the more positive title, while the second emphasizes the central problem of the novel. On the basis of these considerations alone, it is difficult to say which is the better title.

But if his publishers would not allow Trollope to emphasize through his novel's title the steady part of Mr. Harding's vocation, he found other means to make that emphasis. It is interesting to note, for instance, that Trollope, up until Bold's interruption of Mr. Harding's concert in chapter 3, generally gives Mr. Harding the title of precentor, not warden. As soon as Mr. Harding begins to doubt his position, however, Trollope starts calling him "the warden." And the story ends with a reference to the two names: "It was long before the people of Barchester forgot to call Mr. Harding by his long well-known name of Warden. It had become so customary to say Mr. Warden, that it was not easily dropped. 'No, no,' he always says when so addressed, 'not warden now, only precentor.' "

But if by the end of the novel Mr. Harding has divested himself of the wardenship—rid himself of an ambiguous part of his vocation—his action in so doing has not been entirely negative, for Mr. Harding is at the novel's end once again an active pastor of a parish.

It is true that St. Cuthbert's is anything but an imposing living, being "the smallest possible parish, containing a part of the Cathedral Close and a few old houses adjoining." And the church itself "is no bigger than an ordinary room—perhaps twenty-seven feet long by eighteen wide—but," Trollope adds significantly, "still it is a perfect church." And in that perfect church, Mr. Harding, his vocation having been purified and perfected, "performs afternoon service every Sunday, and administers the Sacrament once in every three months."

The Good Shepherd of the New Testament lays down his life for his sheep. If Mr. Harding does not literally lay down his life, he certainly lays down his way of life, or a good part of it. And though he gives up the wardenship for the sake of his conscience rather than, directly, for the sake of his sheep, there can be no doubt that Mr. Harding is a better shepherd at the end of the novel than he was at the beginning. And if Hiram's bedesman do not profit from the reform movement but rather suffer from it (though Trollope was in favor of reform, he was aware of the price that must be paid for it; thus he styled himself not simply a liberal but a conservative-liberal), the parishioners of St. Cuthbert's are certainly fortunate in having gained such a pastor.

The action of *The Warden* can be looked at in several ways. It is possible to say, for instance, that the novel's central action is the giving-up of the wardenship. Looked at more positively, however, the action is the perfecting of Mr. Harding's vocation. That process proceeds steadily and inevitably through the course of the novel. It begins in chapter 3 with John Bold's interruption of the precentor's concert with the announcement of his plan to look into the carrying-out of John Hiram's will; it continues in the same chapter with Mr. Harding's first real doubts about his position as warden; it proceeds in chapter 5 when Mr. Harding, after the archdeacon's talk to the bedesmen, becomes "all but fixed in his resolve that some great step must be taken"; it proceeds further in chapter 9 when, after he receives news of Sir Abraham Haphazard's opinion, Mr. Harding "resolved in his misery and enthusiasm that he could with pleasure, if he were allowed, give up his place, abandon his pleasant home, leave the hospital, and live poorly, happily, and with an unsullied name, on the small remainder of his means"; it receives but a temporary setback when Mr. Harding, after listening to the arch-deacon's irrefutable logic, "went home, resolved to bear it all—

ignominy, suspense, disgrace, self-doubt, and heart-burning—and to do as those would have him, who he still believed were most fit and most able to counsel him aright"; it proceeds again with his suffering in the garden in chapter 10 and speeds up when Eleanor advises her father to " 'give it up, papa' "; it continues through Mr. Harding's decision in chapter 13 that " 'I have no right to be here,' " through the suffering of his long day in London (chap. 16), through the interview with Sir Abraham Haphazard (chap. 17), and through the archdeacon's objections in chapter 18; it culminates in the formal resignation of chapter 19 and concludes in the final two chapters with Mr. Harding's leaving the hospital, the bedesmen, and his old home in order to begin his new life, with lodgings in Barchester, as pastor of St. Cuthbert's. There can be little doubt that the central action of the novel is coherent and unified.

The Warden has but two plots. The first and major plot bears the central action, the giving-up of the wardenship. The second plot bears the love story, the John Bold–Eleanor Harding romance and eventual marriage. Since Bold is obviously a major character in both plots, he makes an obvious connection between them. The two plots, however, have more important connections than this obvious one.

Because the resolution of the major plot depends entirely on the warden's decision, a decision which he makes "in a court of conscience" and independently of all considerations and influences except the question of the justice, not the legality, of his retaining the wardenship, it appears that there can be no causal connection between the two plots, and the appearance is partially correct. Both Eleanor and John try to resolve the warden's problem for him, Eleanor using John's love for her as a club to compel him to give up his lawsuit, and he actually giving it up. But since the dropping of the suit does not get at the real problem, Mr. Harding ignores it. But though Eleanor is wrong in supposing that the dropping of the suit will solve her father's problem and therefore she might have spared her using her influence on Bold, before she does use that influence, she tells her father not to hesitate to give up the wardenship on her account: " 'Do you think that I cannot be happy without a pony-carriage and a fine drawing-room? Papa, I never can be happy here, as long as there is a question as to your honour in staying here.' " Such a declaration would make Mr. Harding's decision somewhat easier, and if he might have hesitated to resign for fear that he would put his daughter in conditions less favorable for marriage, Eleanor's declaration would have removed that cause for hesitation. One may say, then, that there is a causal, if negative, connection between the two plots at least to the extent that Eleanor does not let her love affair affect the advice she gives to her father.

If the strict causal connection between the two plots seems somewhat tenuous, the relationship between them in terms of foreshadowing and preparation, in terms of making the resignation seem even more necessary and inevitable than it really is, is clearer and firmer. In chapter 11, "Iphigenia," Eleanor forces Bold to promise to give up his proceedings against her father. She supposes that the price of such an unusual action will be her romance with Bold. As things turn out, the emotion she expends in forcing the reformer away from his project only intensifies their love for each other and precipitates the declaration of his passion. Though Trollope admits that "unmarried ladies of thirty-five" would have foreseen the outcome of Eleanor's interview with Bold, since they know "that young women on their knees before their lovers are sure to get kissed," he by no means questions the purity of Eleanor's motivation. The important thing is that though at the end of the chapter "the altar on the shore of the modern Aulis reeked with no sacrifice," Eleanor fully intended the sacrifice, fully intended to give up her lover for the sake of her father.

Eleanor does not have to give up her lover, but her lover does give up his proceedings against the warden. Bold's sacrifice, though ultimately futile because the warden pays no attention to it, is real enough and painful enough. Bold suffers most fully when he enters the lairs (those studies which, as Sherman Hawkins has correctly pointed out, are so much alike) of Dr. Grantly and Tom Towers to announce that he has given up his legal proceedings against the warden. Instead of praise, he receives from the archdeacon salt and vinegar and from Tom Towers pretence and a lecture on the responsibilities of the press. Bold ultimately receives some consolation for his suffering when he marries Eleanor, but before he is connected to the warden through marriage, he is united with him in suffering.

Though the sacrifices of Eleanor and John differ inasmuch as the first is only attempted whereas the second is completed, they are alike insofar as neither is effective in relieving Mr. Harding of the burden of his decision and sacrifice. More important, however, both are alike in preparing the way for the warden's resignation, the third and climactic sacrifice of the novel. As Mr. Harding's giving-up of the wardenship is the means by which he perfects his vocation, that resignation is the most nearly perfect self-sacrifice of a series of such sacrifices in the novel. Although the first two sacrifices, both originating in the secondary plot, cannot be said to affect the primary plot by means of causality, they beautifully foreshadow the climactic event of the primary plot and, by so doing, unite the two plots in a significant fashion.

If the subplot is united with the main plot in a significant fashion and if the main plot bears the central action, which action is unified and coherent, one may still wonder about the function of certain characters, scenes, and situations which belong to the main plot. From one point of view, the function of such characters as Tom Towers, Dr. Anticant, Mr. Sentiment, and Sir Abraham Haphazard is quite apparent. These characters exist to put pressure on the warden and to increase that pressure so that Mr. Harding can see clearly that the problem will not go away by itself and that he will have to make a decision about his position. And from another point of view, another function of Towers, Anticant, and Sentiment appears. They exist so that Trollope can attack the second evil which he set out to deal with in the novel. He says in the *Autobiography* that though he had been much struck by the first evil, the misuse of charitable funds by churchmen, "I had also often been angered by the undeserved severity of the newspapers towards the recipients of such incomes, who could hardly be considered to be the chief sinners in the matter."

But though this second function of some of the minor characters is readily seen in the light of the *Autobiography*, the important question is: Was Trollope successful in pursuing this second function within the artistic framework of the whole novel? By the time he came to write the *Autobiography*, Trollope had come to feel that he was not successful. A study of the novel, however, shows differently.

If the central action of the novel is the perfecting of Mr. Harding's vocation, the subject or theme of vocation is important everywhere in the work. If Mr. Harding figures in the novel as a man who comes to live up fully to his vocation, most of the other characters illuminate him by contrast. It is true that a few of the minor figures—Chadwick, the bishop's steward, for instance, and Bunce, the good bedesman, Mr. Harding's unofficial subwarden—

are what they should be, but most of the other characters deviate in some fashion from their calling. Without attempting an exhaustive survey of such deviations, one may, in a reasonable amount of space, note the more significant failures of vocation.

John Bold, the Barchester Reformer, is by profession a surgeon. Sherman Hawkins has pointed out the appropriateness of this profession for the kind of reformer Bold is: "Since the reformer undertakes to cure abuses . . . he becomes a doctor. But not a general practitioner like Dr. Thorne, who, in a later novel, acts as a healer of a sick society: Bold's vocation of surgeon implies a more drastic, painful, and destructive therapy." Equally important as the fact that Bold is by profession a surgeon, however, is the fact that Bold, though he has put up in Barchester "a large brass plate with 'John Bold, Surgeon,' on it," does not really practice his profession; for though "John Bold is a clever man, and would, with practice, be a clever surgeon . . . he has got quite into another line of life." John Bold is a reformer, then, at the price of his profession. He is by no means a model surgeon.

But as a reformer Bold, as his name suggests, is not model either. Trollope does hesitate to call him a demagogue, "for I hardly know how extreme must be a man's opinions before he can be justly so called," but he makes it clear that Bold as a reformer leaves something to be desired:

> I fear that he is too much imbued with the idea that he has a special mission for reforming. It would be well if one so young had a little more diffidence himself, and more trust in the honest purposes of others—if he could be brought to believe that old customs need not necessarily be evil, and that changes may possibly be dangerous; but no, Bold has all the ardour and all the self-assurance of a Danton, and hurls his anathemas against time-honoured practices with the violence of a French Jacobin.

But Bold's lack of moderation is probably not an unmixed evil, for in some situations a crudely carried-out reform might be preferable to no reform at all, and Trollope does admit that "there is something to be admired in the energy with which he devotes himself to remedying evil and stopping injustice." In any event, Bold's major failing in what may be called his second vocation, reforming, comes about not through his zeal for reform but through his passion for Eleanor Harding. Though Bold's giving up his law suit at Eleanor's request does not solve Mr. Harding's problem for him, it does put an end to Bold's activity as a reformer. Perhaps if he had lived Bold might have returned to reforming, but since Trollope killed him off in the novelistic time between *The Warden* and *Barchester Towers*, one must conclude that his career as a reformer was little more distinguished than his career as a surgeon. Perhaps, while he lived, he was a model husband.

Dr. Grantly, who almost became friendly with Bold, his brother-in-law, before that young man died, has every appearance of being more successful in his vocation than Bold in either of his. Trollope's description of the archdeacon certainly portrays him as a successful man: "His heavy eyebrows, large open eyes, and full mouth and chin expressed the solidity of his order; the broad chest, amply covered with fine cloth, told how well to do was its estate; one hand ensconced within his pocket, evinced the practical hold which our mother church keeps on her temporal possessions." The only trouble is that this embodiment of the church establishment is more notable for his worldly than spiritual success, for though he is by no means, as a French critic put it, "le pharisien clérical au complet, le Machiavel de sacristie" (Émile Montégut), he falls considerably short of the ideal of the Good Shepherd. Mr. Harding, who does come close to that ideal, having almost instinctively taken refuge in Westminster Abbey, reflects that here he can be safe from the archdeacon, for "the archdeacon would certainly not come to morning service at Westminster Abbey, even though he were in London." Trollope could hardly have pointed up more sharply than this the essential difference between the two clergymen. At the end of the novel he does try hard to give the archdeacon his due but the best he can do for the archdeacon is to conclude that "on the whole, the Archdeacon of Barchester is a man doing more good than harm,—a man to be furthered and supported, though perhaps also to be controlled." The Archdeacon of Barchester could be worse—he could be a Pharisee or a Machiavelli—but he should be better. Despite his outward appearance of success, the archdeacon finally cannot be adjudged a man who comes close to fulfilling the ideals of his profession.

The archdeacon's sons cannot (at least in this novel) be taken very seriously as sons, but as, in James's words, "little effigies of three distinguished English bishops of that period," they play proper roles in a novel of vocation. If the Church itself, as symbolized by the archdeacon, is too worldlywise, then it is appropriate to bring to light with specific detail examples of that wisdom as manifested in three of her distinguished sons, three real bishops, all clever boys who "gave good promise of being well able to meet the cares and trials of the world." It is possible that the carrying-out of the satire on Bishops Blomfield, Phillpotts, and Wilberforce may strike some readers as being rather heavy-handed (as some of the echoes of *The Rape of the Lock* may seem rather clumsily contrived), but from the point of view of theme and structure there can be little question about the legitimacy and appropriateness of the three portraits.

The portraits of Dr. Anticant and Mr. Sentiment are also attacks upon real men, but instead of being gratuitous assaults, these portraits allow Trollope to extend his range and to emphasize the fact that in mid-Victorian England churchmen were by no means alone in misusing or failing to live up to their vocations. Of the two men, Trollope portrays Mr. Sentiment (Dickens) as being the far more effective writer. From one point of view, he knows his business very well and acts accordingly: "The artist who paints for the million must use glaring colours, as no one knew better than Mr. Sentiment when he described the inhabitants of his almshouse; and the radical reform which has now swept over such establishments has owed more to the twenty numbers of Mr. Sentiment's novel, than to all the true complaints which have escaped from the public for the last half century." In contrast to the twenty numbers of Mr. Sentiment's novel, "Dr. Anticant's monthly pamphlet on the decay of the world did not receive so much attention as his earlier works." Differing in effectiveness, the writing of the two men is alike in this respect, however: inasmuch as it pretends to represent the real world, it is irresponsible. Coming as they do two-thirds of the way through the novel, the pictures which *Modern Charity* and *The Almshouse* present of Mr. Harding must strike the reader as simply false. And since neither Dr. Anticant nor Mr. Sentiment has bothered to become acquainted with Mr. Harding in order to ascertain what kind of man he really is, it is no wonder that the pictures are false and the writing irresponsible.

One might argue, of course, that the essayist-prophet and the novelist are quite right in not allowing matters of fact to impinge upon the purity of their visions, but Trollope would apparently not agree with such an argument. In any event, there can be no question at all about the third target of Trollope's satire in chapter 15, for Tom Towers is not a seer but a practicing journalist. If anyone should get his facts straight, he should. But the fact is that Towers is pictured as no more interested in reality, in the real Mr. Harding, than are Anticant and Sentiment. Instead of paying attention to Bold's testimony on behalf of Mr. Harding's character, Towers first pleads ignorance, suggesting that he does not know who has been writing the articles in the *Jupiter* attacking Mr. Harding. When pressed by Bold, Towers turns upon him and lectures him upon the freedom and responsibility of the press. " 'The public is defrauded,' said he, 'whenever private considerations are allowed to have weight.' " But the public is also defrauded when the press has little regard for the truth, "when," as Trollope says in his own voice, the public "is purposely misled."

"Poor public!" Trollope continues; "how often it is misled! against what a world of fraud has it to contend!" Trollope by no means intends that this world of fraud should be seen as confined to the world of journalism, for politicians too can and do misuse their powers for their own ends. Here is how Sir Abraham Haphazard's Convent Custody Bill, the one hundred and seventh clause of which "ordered the bodily searching of nuns for Jesuitical symbols by aged clergymen," functions in the novel: it is an instance of political fraud—a successful such instance, for "the innocent Irish fell into the trap as they always do, and whiskey and poplins became a drug in the market." As Hawkins notes, the Church comes off rather well in comparison with the powers of this world: "Its misuse of worldly goods is far less vicious than the World's misuse of religion: witness Sir Abraham and the 'Convent Custody Bill.' "

Sir Abraham, besides affording Trollope the occasion to extend his satire to the world of politics, stands in the novel as a horrible example of the successful man of the world. He is both self-made and self-occupied. "He knew every one whom to know was an honour, but he was without a friend. . . . He never quarrelled with his wife, but he never talked to her—he never had time to talk, he was so taken up with speaking." Between such a man and Mr. Harding there is a world of difference. It is no wonder that the successful man of the world cannot understand the decision by which the clergyman perfects his vocation; it is no wonder that Sir Abraham labels Mr. Harding's decision to resign the wardenship as "sheer Quixotism." It is no wonder, and it is quite fitting that Trollope should bring together these two men at a climactic moment of the novel, for the man who has lost his life through his vocation serves as a climactic contrast to the man who gives up his old life in order to find new life in his vocation.

Jerome Thale has observed that "the Trollope novel depends upon parallels, contrasts, repetitions with slight variations. These things, which are present to some extent in any novel, become in Trollope the method of organization." *The Warden* certainly contains the kind of parallels, contrasts, and repetitions which Thale has in mind. The contrast between Sir Abraham and Mr. Harding is not a solitary instance of the use of such a device in the novel. The unity in suffering which binds together Bold and Mr. Harding has already been noted, as have the two sacrifices which lead up to Mr. Harding's resignation. Further parallels could be pointed out—for instance, the bishop's holding firm against the archdeacon's pressure after Mr. Harding has done the same—but it should already be sufficiently clear that *The Warden*, besides being a novel with a unified central action, is a work containing a high degree of unity both of theme and situation. It does have James's "classic roundness," though the "blemish on its fair face" which he saw is no blemish. *The Warden* may have its faults but if it does, they are not structural.

Rebecca West believes that *The Warden's* "very slight degree of failure is surely due to its attempt to be at one and the same time a realistic novel and a satire," and there may be something to her statement. Certainly the realism with which Mr. Harding's struggle of conscience is depicted should not obscure the satirical intent of the novel and its general concern with vocation. One wonders, however, whether *Lycidas* would be a worse poem if Milton had projected the grief at King's death as more heartfelt. It seems unlikely, as it seems unlikely that the moral center of a satirical novel need be drawn in the same way as the objects of the satire. It is just possible that the novel which is able to attack, with success and at the same time, two opposite abuses may also succeed in combining realism with satire in the right amounts. *The Warden*, in any event, remains rounded and structurally unblemished.

Barchester Towers: The Comedy of Change

U. C. Knoepflmacher

Like all the Victorian novels discussed in [*Laughter and Despair*], *Barchester Towers* draws the reader into a fictive reality that simultaneously imitates and counters the disjunctions of the actual world. As representative of that disjunctive external world, Slope the Intruder acts as the novelist's agent as well as his antagonist. Though rendered laughable and, at the end, made to seem quite innocuous, Mr. Slope thus is cast in essentially the same role as those more serious perturbers, Thackeray's Becky Sharp and Conrad's Vladimir. In *Barchester Towers*, however, the placid pastoral world Trollope has invented ceases to be convulsed as soon as this outside agitator is removed; in *Vanity Fair* and in *The Secret Agent*, on the other hand, Becky Sharp and Vladimir merely mirror the dominant ways of an unstable and unsettling Vanity Fair. To use Trollope's quietistic comedy as the starting point for a progression that will immediately take us to Thackeray's grim panorama of flux and vanity and lead us, eventually, to Conrad's terrifying approximation of chaos may therefore seem an odd choice.

There is, furthermore, an odd breach in chronology: *Barchester Towers* was published in 1857, ten years after both *Vanity Fair* and *Wuthering Heights*. Compared with either of these works, Trollope's novel seems curiously antiquated in outlook as well as in its artistic form. Whereas Thackeray's satiric vignettes of urban mobility and

From *Laughter and Despair: Readings in Ten Novels of the Victorian Era*. © 1971 by the Regents of the University of California. University of California Press, 1971.

Emily Brontë's romance about the decay of two country houses yield a vision of irreconcilables, Trollope's mildly disarrayed world seems all too easily restored. Barchester life proves to be only slightly affected by the rapid shifts of London, Trollope's inconstant "world at large." While Thackeray and Brontë seriously question the values on which modern civilization is predicated, Trollope relies on his notions of eighteenth-century decorum to placate his desire for order. To protect themselves against some of the same insecurities which Trollope fears, Thackeray and Emily Brontë were led to experiment with new fictional forms. Although, in a way, Trollope too is an improviser, his adaptation of Fielding and Smollett for his purposes hardly seemed innovative by 1857. As early as 1836–37, in *The Pickwick Papers*, Dickens had tried to evoke the quaintness of the eighteenth-century in order to lend stability to that deranged and dehumanized world he was to portray with increasing intensity in his later work.

Why, then, should we begin with Trollope? It is precisely because he is so successful in his game, because he manages to delude us into thinking that he has provided us with nothing more than a throwback to an earlier, uncomplicated age, that his accomplishment is unique. His world of purgative laughter and complete poetic justice serves as an impregnable bastion against the same confusion that his contemporaries could not manage to screen as easily or as completely. Trollope does not, however, fence out that confusion; quite to the contrary, he invites it into his archaic bastion just as Miss Thorne admits "the world at large" into the walled interior of Ullathorne Court. Within the confines of *Barchester Towers* the same forces which other novelists magnified into gigantic proportions are starved into a Lilliputian shape. Trollope welcomes chaos because, through the mock-heroic and burlesque, he can reduce it and laugh it away.

The same tension underlying the novels we shall consider [elsewhere] thus exists in *Barchester Towers* in a simpler and more pristine shape. There is an alternation between threat and relief, between the fear of disintegration and the pleasure brought through the return of harmony. Compelled by Trollope to identify with Mr. Harding, we soon share his sense of dislocation, the anxiety that comes with the insider's displacement by the outsider. In *Barchester Towers*, however, Mr. Harding's alienation is at best potential; it is handled lightly by the jovial narrator whose presence assures us that relief is in sight. In other novels, where the fluctuations between laughter and despair take on far more somber hues, the discordances that vex Mr. Harding cannot as readily be reconstituted into harmony. In these novels patterns similar to those employed by Trollope will recur, yet with a quite altered emphasis. Thus, the fear of dislocation we share with Mr. Harding becomes intensified when his place is taken by a Maggie Tulliver or a Jude; the pleasure we derive from the expulsion of a Silas Wegg or Vladimir must reconcile us to changes that are far more irreparable than the slight alterations left in the wake of Mr. Slope's departure. The homogeneity that reigns at the end of *Barchester Towers*, though sought by the other novelists, can seldom be duplicated. In Mr. Arabin, Mr. Harding finds a son in his own image. Such continuity is impossible in all those novels which stress the gap between fathers and children as a metaphor for the disruption so strongly felt by the Victorians. Even in those novels where there are similar attempts at continuity, the differences are palpable: Fred Vincy fashions himself after his father-in-law and Hareton becomes a humanized Heathcliff, but both are secondary figures, shaded by more pathetic counterparts.

Trollope himself was to write the far more gloomy, Thackera-yan, *The Way We Live Now* in 1875. In 1857, however, he fortified himself and his readers by writing a novel he might well have entitled "The Way We Still May Live." In *Barchester Towers* he calmly defused the despair that led other Victorian novelists to defend themselves through constructs that were far bolder, but also far more uneven in form.

I

Thematically as well as artistically, *Barchester Towers* relies on the juxtaposition of the ostensible and the implied. Throughout the novel, the narrator distinguishes between facade and motive, between what he calls the "outer" and the "inner" man. He extends this distinction not only to dissemblers like Mr. Slope but even to characters like Eleanor Bold or Mr. Arabin, who, though far less fallible, are only imperfectly aware of their own inner motives. It is significant, in this connection, that Trollope should employ the mythical domain of Ullathorne to disengage the "inner" from the "outer" self. At Ullathorne, which rigorously filters the influx of the world at large, an honesty is possible which exists neither in London nor in Barchester. The small sphere of the Thornes seems hopelessly limited; it refines even further the stylized world of Trollope's comedy. Still, it is precisely because, in it, the characters "see so very very little" that they also learn to recognize what may be most genuine and enduring.

It is at Ullathorne that Bertie Stanhope reveals truths he would not have dared to utter in Barchester; at Ullathorne, where Eleanor tells her father what she would not openly admit in Dr. Grantly's house; at Ullathorne, where the stiff Mr. Arabin finally manages to say "Eleanor" instead of "Mrs. Bold." At Ullathorne even Mr. Slope is led to abandon his indirections. He drops his ambiguous verbal allusions and puts his arm around Eleanor's waist. And she retaliates in kind: "Quick as thought, she raised her little hand and dealt him a box on the ear with such right good will, that it sounded among the trees like a miniature thunderclap" (chap. 40). The action, like many other actions in Trollope's world, is mock-heroic, but unlike the fulminations of the *Jupiter* or Mr. Grantly's oaths and imprecations, this miniature thunderclap, delivered by a dainty hand, is genuine. Ullathorne may be ludicrous, as outlandish as the Thornes themselves. Its very quaintness, however, allows Trollope to convert it into the center of feeling of his novel.

What seems salient and prominent in *Barchester Towers* is invariably not so. As we saw [elsewhere], the book's opening chapter ostensibly dramatizes the aspirations and plight of Archdeacon Grantly, whereas its primary effect is to introduce us to the undramatic, but truly central, figure of Grantly's father-in-law. Ostensibly again, the novel's main plot line seems to be built around the wardenship of Hiram's Hospital. Yet the competition for this office is secondary; it is created by Trollope solely for the purpose of introducing complications that become so absorbing that the wardenship itself is made utterly insignificant. Even these complications, which presumably depict the battle between two clerical factions, soon turn out to conceal something else: the battle of the sexes.

The question of "Who Will Be the New Warden?" replaces, after the first chapter, the quickly answered question of "Who Will Be the New Bishop?" Trollope's handling of the plot soon makes this second question seem less and less compelling. The reader immediately sympathizes with Mr. Harding, whose claims to the position he had lost in *The Warden* seem rightful. When Mr. Harding, cleverly outmaneuvered by Slope, feels displaced and thrown out on the "rubbish cart" as outmoded dross, we are all the more drawn to his side. Yet the reader's sympathies are dampened as soon as we discover that, by supporting Harding, we are also supporting his vociferous son-in-law who vows that "we" must battle for the wardenship. We waver in our allegiances. The reader knows that Grantly's schemes to import Mr. Arabin and Dr. Gwynne to fight under his banner are meaningless: in the interim, the fickle Mr. Slope has altered his plans, having discovered that Mr. Harding is the father of a daughter as rich as she is beautiful. When new participants jump into the fray—with the enraged Mrs. Quiverful pleading for the intervention of Mrs. Proudie in the name of her fourteen little arrows—the contest for a position no longer desired by Mr. Harding himself becomes ludicrous. The three characters who ought to be most directly involved in the action—the bishop empowered to award the position and the two candidates for it—passively stand at the sidelines, displaced by a trio to whom the position itself is relevant only as a test for their strength. Thus, Dr. Proudie hovers insecurely between his secretary and his wife; Mr. Quiverful between Mr. Slope and his own wife; Mr. Harding between Slope and Grantly. Ultimately, Mr. Harding does not at all mind having the appointment go to his rival; diverted by other thoughts, he has become far more apprehensive about his daughter's status than his own. Quiverful, who really needs the job, thus gets it by default. The reader too has been diverted. The alliances, attacks, counterattacks, and capitulations have turned out to be far more absorbing than their prime mover—the wardenship itself. We care about Trollope's endless improvisations; separate episodes, separate conversations, separate character sketches and vignettes have engrossed us completely. The disputed wardenship has been but a ploy to engage us in the battle of the clergy.

Yet this battle, too, turns out to be a sham. Though Grantly declares war against Slope after their first and only meeting, the promised combat between the two men never takes place. For all his heroic speeches and posturings, Grantly is as wary a combatant as the enemy whose indirections he despises. He refuses to meet Slope head-on. Instead, he addresses his cohort, marshals it through meaningless exercises, and imports Arabin as a surefire ally, an "ecclesiastical knight before whose lance Mr. Slope was to fall and bite the dust" (chap. 47). The new paladin's fame rests solely on his rhetorical powers as a polemicist; Arabin has faced Slope only in the pages of a newspaper. When he and the bishop's chaplain meet at last, it is not as public jousters, but rather as two men privately competing for Eleanor Bold. Mr. Harding's public cause has been all but forgotten (indeed, Grantly and his allies do not even know that Slope, too, now wants Harding to become the warden). When Grantly brings in still another champion, Dr. Gwynne, the master of Lazarus College, neither he nor that gentleman suspects that the enemy they want (but do not dare) to fight openly has already fallen out of favor with the bishop.

Hence, at the end of the novel Mr. Grantly's inflated sense of victory is ridiculous. He has never met Slope directly, yet he assures himself that somehow he has led his forces to a triumph of epic proportions. The narrator slyly undermines the belligerent clergyman's self-aggrandizement. He first renders Grantly's thoughts in all their pomposity: "The archdeacon had trampled upon Mr. Slope, and had lifted to high honours the young clergyman whom he had induced to quit the retirement and comfort of the university." The narrator then adds, in his own voice: "So at least the archdeacon thought; though, to speak sooth, not he, but circumstances, had trampled on Mr. Slope" (chap. 52). The implications are clear. The archdeacon takes credit for a battle he has waged only in his own mind. For Slope, and Slope alone, has been the novel's actor. It is he who first disrupts the harmony of Barchester and he again who, by overreaching himself, brings about the restoration of peace and order.

In a tongue-in-cheek improvisation on *Paradise Lost*, Trollope's narrator tells us that every novel should have its male and female angels, as well as its male and female devils (chap. 26). Dr. Grantly unequivocally regards Slope as "a messenger from Satan." The narrator's more jocular use of demonic allusions throughout the story invites us to regard the chaplain as a ludicrous cousin of the conniver who, in *Paradise Lost*, forced God's angels into a similar position of reaction. Still, the archdeacon who prides himself on having trampled on his adversary is by no means one of the novel's "male angels." In *Paradise Lost* war was the fault of a single party; in Trollope's mock-epic world, Slope's "pride" is very much shared by Grantly. In Milton's heaven, the good angels become infected by Satan's unfair tactics; mountains began to fly all over the place. In Barchester, neither a heaven nor a paradise, the Grantlyites become even more confused. In Trollope's travesty an oily, carrot-headed minister with sweaty hands replaces Milton's heroic Satan, molehills replace flying mountains, and a well-applied slap is substituted for Michael's fiery sword. This unheroic world contains no peerless angels.

Like a good tactician, Mr. Slope knows how to exploit the element of surprise. He deliberately provokes the clergymen who have gathered in the cathedral to listen to his first sermon. Like Milton's fiend, who spoke in "ambiguous words," the crafty secretary speaks in an "ambiguous manner" (chap. 6); yet his words are sufficiently unambiguous to reveal his objectives to his captive audience. Mr. Slope takes his sermon from St. Paul's text: "Study to show thyself approved unto God, a workman that needeth not to be ashamed, rightly dividing the word of truth" (2 Tim. 2:15). Hiding behind both the authority of the Scriptures and the authority of the bishop who sits behind him, he uses this authority for divisive purposes. The new doctrines he advances merely mask his personal ambitions. (Mr. Arabin's text at St. Ewold, in Ullathorne, is the exact reverse of Slope's: "Whosoever transgresseth and abideth not in the doctrine of God, hath no God.")

Like his heroic cousin, "the damp, sandy-haired, saucer-eyed, red-fisted Mr. Slope" at first seems to exert a distinct power over "the female breast." The party now forming in Barchester on his "side of the question" consists "chiefly of ladies" (chap. 7). Satan, in the guise of the serpent, raised Eve's expectations by promising her unforseen changes; this minister, who knows and uses "the wiles of the serpent" (chap. 8), promises to alter the "old humdrum way" of Barchester. The ladies of his party are willing to lend him their ears: "People in advance of their age now had new ideas, and it was high time that Barchester should go in advance" (chap. 7). Still, Mr. Slope's acquired power is precarious. The narrator risks a prediction: "Could Mr. Slope have adapted his manners to men as well as to women, could he ever have learnt the ways of a gentleman, he might have risen to great things" (chap. 8). The words are rather ironic, for it is by women and not by men that Mr. Slope will be defeated. Wounded by Eleanor's smart slap, deflated by Signora Neroni, and stripped of his powers by Mrs. Proudie, the novel's "male devil" becomes incongruous in his role. He is a Satan defeated by Eve.

The pride that caused both Satan's and Adam's fall is neatly distributed among all men in Trollope's comic universe. To remind us that Grantlyism and its quarrelsome flag-bearer are subject to Mr.

Slope's own flaws, Trollope engages in a superb parody of Milton's epic in chapter 7, "The Dean and Chapter Take Counsel." In *Paradise Lost* the fallen angels called a counsel to determine whether to fight God openly or with guile; but in the face of an all-seeing and omnipotent God, their heroism was futile. Trollope plays with a similar situation but deliberately reverses the parties: it is the "good" party, stung by Slope's sermon, who meet to hold a "high debate together as to how Mr. Slope should be put down." Milton's scene is antiheroic; the warriors whose appeal to arms is so sonorous are secretly aware of their impotence. Trollope's scene exaggerates this same absurdity: the congregation of clergymen do not dare to engage an enemy shielded by the authority of their bishop. The best they can do is to hold on to their own self-respect. Just as Milton's angels vainly exulted in their former titles, Powers, Thrones, Dominions, so do dean, prebendary, vicar, and canon cling to their hierarchical positions. In Pandemonium, Satan rose to announce a safe course of action against God's divine authority; in the deanery, where there are neither archangels nor archfiends, it is the archdeacon who manfully tries to rally his dispirited forces. His introduction carries a Miltonic ring:

> Then up rose Dr. Grantly; and, having
> Thus collected the scattered wisdom
> Of his association, spoke forth with words
> Of deep authority.

But this epic note is quickly undermined by the narrator: "When I say up rose the archdeacon, I speak of the inner man, which then sprang up to more immediate action, for the doctor, had, bodily, been standing all along with his back to the dean's empty fire-grate, and the tails of his frock supported over his two arms. His hands were in his breeches pocket."

Milton's Satan asserted his power over his fallen band by promising to fight single-handed the warfare they eschew; eagerly, the fallen angels give up their authority to him. The scene in the deanery ends with a similar submission to Mr. Grantly: "There was much more discussion among the learned conclave, all of which, of course, ended in obedience to the archdeacon's commands. They had too long been accustomed to his rule to shake it off so soon." Trollope's parody thus reinforces Milton's insight: in the face of change, men, like angels, gladly abdicate their freedom to those who promise them a restoration of their former prerogatives. Both scenes end with an illusion: the members of the fallen party, aware of their own inability to reverse change, rejoice in the notion that their leader will defy the authority they fear. In *Paradise Lost* this illusion is nurtured by Satan's majestic speech—a speech that will be followed by immediate action: the flight through Chaos and the Portals of Hell. In *Barchester Towers,* however, Mr. Grantly will never match words with actions. Instead, he merely indulges in vituperation. When he declares Slope's behavior to have been abominable, his pliant audience readily agrees: " 'Abominable,' groaned the dean. 'Abominable,' muttered the meagre doctor. 'Abominable,' re-echoed the chancellor." Even the pacific Mr. Harding is swept along: " 'I really think it was,' said Mr. Harding." The group's defiance, however, remains secret; Grantlyism is but a posture. Instead of an active hero, fighting an impossible cause, we are presented with a frocked clergyman whose hands are in his breeches pocket for the remainder of the novel.

Absolute perfection does not exist in Trollope's world. "Human ends," we are told at one point, "must be attained by human means." And these means are, as we are so often reminded, highly limited. Dr. Grantly may pride himself on his martial skills and import a retinue of champions, but his grandiose designs, like his verbiage, are inevitably deflated by the narrator: "Dr. Gwynne was the *Deus ex machina* who was to come upon the Barchester stage, and bring about deliverance from these terrible evils. But how can melodramatic *dénouements* be properly brought about, how can vice and Mr. Slope be punished, and virtue and the archdeacon be rewarded, while the avenging god is laid up with the gout?" (chap. 34). In the epic world of *Paradise Lost,* God is omniscient and omnipotent, even if He sits out the battle for a while. In a world where gods are laid up by the gout, the outcome of the contest between virtue and vice depends on the circumstances contrived by the novelist. And the circumstances which trample Mr. Slope into the ground take the shape of Eleanor, the signora, and Mrs. Proudie rather than that of the fierce archdeacon.

II

The real battle fought in Barchester is not the short-lived struggle between "Proudieism" and "Grantlyism" but rather the more elementary contest waged between men and women. While

Mr. Grantly's fanfare is ostentatious, the skirmishes between the sexes are mostly conducted away from the public eye. In Trollope's handling, however, this competition is far more genuine than the empty scuffles of the two clerical factions. The battle of the clergy depends on a parity of power; in the battle of the sexes, however, the combatants are most unevenly matched. In Trollope's delightfully topsy-turvy world, women are by far the stronger sex.

It is Miss Thorne who comments at one point that "now-a-days the gentlemen were all women, and the ladies all men" (chap. 35). The narrator remarks that Charlotte Stanhope, had she been a man, "would have been a very fine young man" (chap. 9). And indeed the reader who comes to *Barchester Towers* expecting to find those delicate, self-effacing creatures we associate with Victorian womanhood will find that none of the Barchester ladies conforms to the stereotype of the frail female in a masculine world. This stereotype has come to be accepted as a historical fact—even though the Victorian era happens to owe its name to the resolute matron who ruled with absolute power for sixty-four years. But whether Trollope relies on fact or fiction, he gains some of his finest comic effects by inverting the traditional roles of the sexes.

From top to bottom, women dominate in Barchester. Everyone in the town knows that Mrs. Proudie rather than her husband is the real bishop. It is to the bishopess therefore that Mrs. Quiverful applies, indignant at her own quivering husband's abject passivity (to get to the bishop's palace, Mrs. Quiverful appears to a farmer's wife, who in turn forces her mate to provide the transportation). At Ullathorne, Miss Thorne, the rural Britomart, arranges the manly sports her brother neglects. She distributes bows and arrows to the toxophilites and personally supervises the construction of the quintain: "She almost wished . . . to get on a saddle and have a tilt at it herself." In the Stanhope family, Charlotte takes over the duties evaded by her indolent father; she rules her weak brother Bertie and almost persuades him to overcome his aversion to the "tyranny" and "deceit" of marriage (chap. 15). Even Susan Grantly is far more influential than her husband realizes. She pretends to be a "pattern of obedience," but values power as much as the archdeacon himself. In battling the Proudieites, she is "as well prepared as her lord to carry on the battle without giving or taking quarter." In fact, she is better prepared: "Mrs. Grantly had lived the life of a wise, discreet, peace-making woman; and the people of Barchester were surprised at the amount of military vigor she displayed as a general of the feminine Grantlyite forces" (chap. 13).

The Barchester males are afraid of the opposite sex. Mr. Harding is terror-stricken at the thought that twelve old women and a matron will be added to the twelve old men at Hiram's Hospital. Mr. Lookaloft is so intimidated by his overbearing wife and daughters that he does not dare to come to the Ullathorne feast. Even Mr. Grantly, that fearless champion, admits that "when a woman is impertinent, one must . . . put up with it." Neither he nor Dr. Gwynne ever dares to challenge the authority of Mrs. Proudie. And Mr. Arabin, forty years old, whose "virgin lips" have never yet "tasted the luxury of a woman's cheek," is far more coy and maidenlike than Eleanor Bold who, for all her refreshing innocence, is the mother of a two-year-old child. When this gentleman finally clasps Eleanor to his bosom, Trollope's narrator wryly comments: "How this was done, whether the doing was with him or her . . . neither of them knew; nor can I declare" (chap. 48).

Unlike his Barchester brethren, Mr. Slope has too little respect for the supremacy of women. (Mr. Slope's disrespect extends to his sovereign: "He cares nothing, one way or the other, for the Queen's supremacy; these to his ears are empty words, meaning nothing" [chap. 4].) Disdainful of those males who, like Proudie or Quiverful or Harding, passively hover between alternatives, he nonetheless finds himself alternating between Eleanor Bold and the enticing Signora Neroni. His indecision proves disastrous. The calculating fortune hunter (who had rejected one of Dr. Proudie's daughters because she lacked a dowry) discovers that his interests are also erotic. His sexuality—betokened by those clammy hands—first manifests itself when he surprises the lovely widow in a semi-innocent sport with her baby son. Smothering her child with kisses, admiring his "lovely legs," Eleanor provokes the child to twist her long glossy hair "hither and thither" (chap. 16). She is confused by Slope's sudden entrance; the chaplain is frankly aroused. His tasteless allusion to her silken tresses shows him to be no Victorian gentleman, but his words do show his desires. He too would like to assault those beautiful long tresses.

It is Signora Neroni, however, who begins to emasculate the chaplain who insisted on being a man in a female world. The smiling signora warns him that "Troilus loved and ceased to be a man." The preacher who had been so able to move the female heart becomes an awkward Ovidian monster seduced by a "couchant goddess": "Mr. Slope, taking the soft fair delicate hand in his, and very soft and fair and delicate it was, bowed over it his huge red head and kissed it. It was a sight to see . . . her hand in his looked like a rose lying among carrots, and when he kissed it he looked as a cow might do on finding such a flower among her food" (chap. 27). The Circe of Barchester is cruel, unsparingly satirical. She exposes the duplicity Slope has so successfully maintained and confronts him with the contradictions between his unworldly religion and his worldly aims: "Why do you want lands and income?" When Slope protests that he has the "natural ambitions of a man," she replies: "Of course you have, and the natural passions; and therefore I say that you don't believe the doctrine you preach." The horrified chaplain is speechless. Checked in his ardor, he returns to try his luck with Eleanor. The widow's slap only increases his frustration: "To him the blow from her little hand was as much an insult as a blow from a man would have been to another. It went direct to his pride. . . . He could almost have struck at her again in his rage. Even the pain was a great annoyance to him" (chap. 40). Like Satan smitten by Michael's sword, Mr. Slope has had his first experience of pain.

Able to divide others to further his ambitions, Slope discovers that his sexual passion has made him a divided man. Recoiling from Eleanor's slap, he turned to Madeline Neroni again, only to be slapped down far more cruelly. For the lady now publicly exposes the gap between his inner desires and outward professions. She reminds this apostle of newness that for once he has lingered too long on the old:

> It's gude to be off with the old love—Mr. Slope,
> Before you are on with the new.—

Escaping her room, Slope finds himself finished off by a third female, Mrs. Proudie, whom he has antagonized beyond repair by his attentions to the signora in Mrs. Proudie's drawing room. Slope comes to rue his passion for the two women to whom he has simultaneously attached himself, but "the pre-eminent place in his soul's hatred was usually allotted to the signora" (chap. 46). By divesting Slope of his mobility, the immobile signora becomes the most powerful figure in the novel. Her physical paralysis, emblematic of the Stanhope lassitude, also has come to represent the triumph of the stationary ways of Barchester. Once regarded as "very like an angel" (chap. 11), the signora whose eyes are "as bright as Lucifer's" (chap. 9) has assumed new characteristics in Mr. Slope's mind: "Whenever he again thought of her in his dreams, it was not as an angel with azure wings. He connected her rather with fire and brimstone" (chap. 46). Although the narrator assures us that Mrs. Proudie was not "all devil" (chap. 26), he does not challenge Slope's imputation. But even if Trollope means the signora to act as the novel's undisputed "female devil," he also makes her the agent of his own godlike dispensation of justice.

Eleanor Bold, the novel's female angel, impresses her superior strength on Mr. Harding and Mr. Arabin by forcing both men to live with her in the deanery; the signora, on the other hand, contributes to the happy ending by forcing the novel's would-be devil to live in perennial exile. In Barchester, Mr. Slope is ignominiously defeated. But outside its confines, in the external world of London, he is allowed to thrive. His marriage to the rich widow of a suger refiner should sweeten the bitterness of the cinders that the signora and Trollope have made him swallow.

III

The peace between the sexes also marks the peace of the clergy—Mr. Proudie submits to his wife; Mr. Quiverful settles in Hiram's Hospital; Mr. Arabin's "virgin lips" meet those of Eleanor; the triumphant Madeline Neroni sets off for new conquests. In comedy, the return to normalcy is signified by marriage. Just as the union of Tom Jones to Sophia Western or Elizabeth Bennett's nuptials to Mr. Darcy repairs the temporary insanity of their world, so here too does marriage become emblematic of the restitution of order. The installment of Mr. Arabin and Eleanor in the deanery of the cathedral assures the reader of a continuity in the ways of Barchester; Mr. Slope's marriage to the sugar refiner's widow signifies that London, "the world at large," will also continue its own way. Each realm returns to its particular mode of life: Barchester will remain conservative, organic; London, innovative and mechanical. Mr. Slope chooses as a seat for his future activities a "church in the vicinity of the *New* Road." His reputation as "one of the most eloquent preachers and pious clergymen in that part of the metropolis" is obviously false (chap. 51, italics added). Although, in Barchester, we have seen the hypocrisy masked by this piety, Slope's future deceptions are unimportant. The bishop's chaplain has served his purpose. Significantly enough, Trollope ends the stories of Slope and of the Proudies well before that of the Barchesterians. He devotes the last two chapters exclusively to their affairs.

For all his importance as a character, Mr. Slope is above all a tool for Trollope's comedy. Like the traditional "Vice" figure of the stage, he challenges an established order. In doing so he stirs up Barchester and induces its inhabitants to become his marionettes. Comedy thrives on making men seem stiff, mechanical, and therefore laughable. Trollope's brand of comedy nonetheless allows us to be kind to his puppets—we like Mr. Harding when he becomes Dr. Grantly's errand boy and sympathize with the former warden precisely when those who espouse his cause talk of him "as though he were a puppet" (chap. 39). Therefore, we rejoice when Mr. Harding, by withdrawing from public life, refuses to be a puppet any longer (the independent Eleanor has throughout rejected the role of marionette); and we rejoice all the more when Mr. Slope, Trollope's deputy puppeteer, becomes himself the puppet of Signora Neroni.

Although the signora's alien manners and mode of thinking clash with those of Barchester, it is she who enables the town to return to its former order. She resembles lethargic Barchester in the sense that both need an outside push—she to be lifted from one place to another, Barchester to be induced to make some progress. Yet this progress is minimal. Without Mr. Slope's urgings, Bishop Proudie will introduce no radical changes to disturb the town's habitual ways. Although the town accepts its new bishop, it is comforted by the thought that he, too, will one day be forced to become a traditionalist when "the new-fangled manners of the age have discovered him to be superannuated" (chap. 51). The changes that have occurred are hardly deplorable. There is a new warden at Hiram's Hospital, and there will be twelve old women and a matron in addition to the twelve male inmates. But this equality of numbers almost seems a male victory in a world in which women do not usually settle for such parity. There is also a new dean to replace Mr. Trefoil, but Francis Arabin, who comes from the Oxford of Newman and Arnold, is hardly a radical. (Oxford was still as much a "venerable seat of Learning, Orthodoxy, and Toryism" in the Victorian era as it had been when Boswell and Johnson visited in 1784.)

At Ullathorne, shortly before declaring their love for each

other, Eleanor and Mr. Arabin comment on their surroundings; their exchange bears quoting in its entirety:

> "Do you like Ullathorne?" said Mr. Arabin, speaking from the safely distant position which he had assumed on the hearth-rug.
> "Yes, indeed, very much!"
> "I don't mean Mr. and Miss Thorne. I know you like them; but the style of the house. There is something about old-fashioned mansions, built as this is, and old-fashioned gardens, that to me is especially delightful."
> "I like everything old-fashioned," said Eleanor; "old fashioned things are so much the honestest."
> "I don't know about that," said Mr. Arabin, gently laughing. "That is an opinion on which very much may be said on either side. It is strange how widely the world is divided on a subject which so nearly concerns us all, and which is so close beneath our eyes. Some think we are quickly progressing towards perfection, while others imagine that virtue is disappearing from the earth."
> "And you, Mr. Arabin, what do you think?" said Eleanor.

The pressed clergyman becomes even more evasive and circuitous than Trollope's own narrator:

> "What do I think, Mrs. Bold?" and then he rumbled his money with his hands in his trowsers pockets, and looked and spoke very little like a thriving lover. "It is the bane of my life that on important subjects I acquire no fixed opinion. I think, and think, and go on thinking; and yet my thoughts are running ever in different directions. I hardly know whether or no we do lean more confidently than our fathers did on those high hopes to which we profess to aspire."
>
> (chap. 48)

In this oblique and characteristically inconclusive fashion, Trollope introduces his own stand on a question that absorbed his age. . . . Like all major Victorian novels, *Barchester Towers* contains a reaction to a quickly shifting world in which traditional values and beliefs are in the process of being challenged, eroded, redefined.

Though Trollope is as equivocal as Mr. Arabin, he clearly sides with Eleanor in preferring "old-fashioned things." The order to which Barchester returns does contain the novelist's own values and assumptions. Human nature is pretty much the same. Though Mr. Grantly may speak of having "girded himself and gone to war," he remains as proud, wistful, and worldly as before. Women will still retain their mastery over men; the merchants of Barchester will still be ruled by self-interest. No man is perfect and no man can be perfected by mere legislation—whether this legislation comes from the Ministry, Parliament, or the *Jupiter*. Change and progress are inevitable, but they must evolve through natural growth rather than through the imposition of arbitrary and mechanical rules. Like Dr. Johnson, Trollope is skeptical about excesses of all kinds, and he believes in social customs and social and religious institutions as the preservers of common sense and order. He is a conservative, not because he necessarily believes in the deterioration of the human race, or because he holds all old things to be better than the new, but rather because he assumes that whatever has been around for a long time has withstood the test of experience. The church music that Mr. Harding loves and Slope attacks has evolved for centuries; to prohibit it seems wanton and arbitrary. Even the "magnificent" violincello which Mr. Grantly, in the flush of victory, bestows on his father-in-law at the end of the novel proves to be useless to the old gentleman. Its "new-fashioned arrangements and expensive additions" baffle him so that he can never use the instrument "with satisfaction to his audience or pleasure to himself" (chap. 53).

Trollope's novel thus depicts a compromise. The superannuated inmates at Hiram's Hospital, confronted with a new warden and a dozen females, exclaim: "We be very old for any change . . . but we do suppose it be all for the best" (chap. 52). The statement can almost be taken as representing the novel's chief theme. In a world of change, the old must yield to the new, yet the new must recognize that experience and tradition contain the guidelines for all future growth. The norms of the past should not be cast on a rubbish cart in the name of "progress."

Despite this commonsense resolution, Trollope nonetheless does indulge in a nostalgic glance at an impossible past. It is no coincidence that the conversation between Eleanor and Arabin should be set in and stimulated by the chimerical world of Ullathorne. In Barchester, Grantlyism is favored by the town's rank and file not out of high principles but simply because the town's merchants do not care for a bishop who spends his money in London. Even those "high-souled ecstatic young ladies of thirty-five" who rally around Mr. Slope come to realize that their opposition to church music is wrong because "their welfare, and the welfare of the place, was connected in some mysterious manner with daily chants and bi-weekly anthems" (chap. 52). In Ullathorne, however, no such self-interest exists.

The Thorne's property is disconnected from merchants and trade and the feudal relationship between squire and tenant is still respected; Miss Thorne personally looks after the children and poor of the parish and fondly regards Harry Greenacre as a "pattern," an "excellent sample of an English yeoman" (chap. 35). The young man, in turn, is willing to act as her knight by tilting at the quintain, unafraid of being "powdered with flour in the service of his mistress" (chap. 36). Only upon being almost brained, does his gallantry abate a trifle. At her *fête champêtre* Miss Thorne entreats her steward, Mr. Plomacy, to be sure to admit all children if "they live near," as well as all the tenants and laborers of the estate. The command proves useless, for soon the park is overrun by apprentices from the city. On capturing one such intruder, Mr. Plomacy decides to eject him from Eden and send him "howling back to a Barchester pandemonium." The steward raises his stick, ready to see "the edict of banishment" carried out by conducting the culprit to the gate. But the justice of this Michael is tempered by mercy: the young man is allowed to stay at the entreaty of Farmer Greenacre. The overjoyed apprentice inwardly swears "that if ever Farmer Greenacre wanted a day's work done for nothing, he was the lad to do it for him" (chap. 39).

A world where people are willing to work for nothing is almost as chimerical as Miss Thorne's stout belief in the existence of men who have long been dead. To live in such a world is unthinkable: though Mr. Arabin and Eleanor are fond of Ullathorne's quaintness, they do not stay at St. Ewold's, but move to Barchester itself. Still, their union has been made possible by the matchmaking Miss Thorne; only upon being transported into the maiden lady's arrested world have the pair recognized their joint affection for old-fashioned mansions and gardens.

IV

In *Barchester Towers* stability is achieved, to a large extent, by Trollope's adoption of the outlook and expression of a much earlier age. Miss Thorne's antiquated literary tastes can almost act as an index for the novels' own heritage: "She spoke of Addison, Swift, and Steele, as though they were still living, regarded De Foe as the best known novelist of his country, and thought of Fielding as a young but meritorious novice in the fields of romance. In poetry, she was familiar with names as late as Dryden, and had once been seduced into reading the 'Rape of the Lock' " (chap. 22).

Trollope's values, too, correspond to those held by earlier writers like Goldsmith or Fielding. A man should cultivate his own garden. He should be modest, have common sense, and perform his duties to the best of his abilities. He should recognize his own flaws and tolerate the imperfections of others. Mr. Harding, we are told in the novel's concluding paragraph, is not a man "who should be toasted at public dinners and spoken of with conventional absurdity as a perfect divine." Instead, he is—what is more important—"a good man without guile," cognizant of his shortcomings and therefore guided by "the precepts which he has striven to learn" (chap. 53).

This portrait of an unworldly clergyman is in the tradition of Fielding's Parson Adams or Goldsmith's Vicar of Wakefield. Not only the values implied in *Barchester Towers* but also the form of Trollope's novel reflect the literary conventions of an earlier age. Its mock-heroic depiction of the battles of the clergy and of the sexes owes much to such works as Swift's *Battle of the Books* or Pope's *Rape of the Lock*. Trollope's narrator is a direct descendant of the digressive commentator and theorist of *Tom Jones*; his episodic plotting is in the manner of Smollett's picaresque fiction. Eleanor's slap, Mrs. Proudie's torn gown, the tilting at the quintain are incidents which could easily have occurred in a novel like *Humphry Clinker*, where the structure lends itself to the portrayal of separate incidents, all vivid and memorable in themselves. The account of the checkered career of Bertie Stanhope (Protestant, Catholic, Jew, and Protestant again), like the thumbnail sketch of Miss Thorne's tastes and opinions, could have come straight out of the periodical essays of Addison and Steele. They render a type: the modern Dandy, the Tory Lady of the old school. Each detail contributes to this type until it is stamped and finished.

Trollope's handling of Bertie differs considerably from the presentation of Dickens's Richard Carstone, Emily Brontë's Lockwood, and George Eliot's Will Ladislaw, all versions of the aimless young man who suffers from *ennui*. Dickens fits Richard into a complex symbolic construct which displays the vanity of man's trust in chance; Brontë uses Lockwood to show the insufficiency of reason in an irrational world of romance; George Eliot penetrates Ladislaw's psychological make-up at the same time that she tries to determine his relation to the society from which he is alienated. Trollope's concerns are less grandiose. Bertie remains a type, laughable in his own right. His idiosyncrasies or "ruling passions" are fascinating in themselves. Each of Trollope's characters is reducible to certain basic humors or vanities. If Bertie stands for a kind of good-humored indolence or purposelessness, the archdeacon is proud, wishful, and worldly, the signora displays a desire for masterhood, Slope wants money, sex, and power. Only combined, can these individual types produce what Trollope at one point calls "the world's deceit" (chap. 44). Laughter can expose that deceit by piercing the social veneers of the outer man.

Trollope's deliberate use of flat characters carries certain limitations. George Eliot would have probed far more deeply into Dr. Grantly's guilt or Mr. Harding's self-doubts; Jane Austen would have exploited the misconceptions of Eleanor Bold and forced the young woman into a gradual recognition of her hasty impressions. Trollope does not altogether avoid the hidden recesses of the "inner man"; but he prefers to rely on inference and suggestion. Passion—so important to the Brontës or to Meredith—is used only mockingly in the figure of Slope, the grotesque, red-haired lover. For Trollope's mode is antiromantic. He eschews the complications of plot that Dickens delighted in and mocks the Gothic romances of Mrs. Radcliffe. In this sense, he is again the exact opposite of those writers who wanted to create a world of mystery and abnormality.

Trollope's limitations are of course his strengths. As a believer in moderation, he mocks excess of any kind. He resorts to parody, for instance, when in sketching Bertie's background he mentions the young man's encounter in Palestine with "one of the family of Sidonia, a most remarkable man" (chap. 9). In Disraeli's *Coningsby* (1844) and *Tancred* (1847), novels which mix their author's political ideals with the extravagances of romance, Sidonia is an exotic, Bedouinlike Jew who instructs two young English aristocrats in the ideals they will implant in their own country. In Trollope's handling, this noble character becomes utterly ridiculous. This signora wants to see the mysterious stranger who has so affected Bertie; she wants to have him at her feet. When Sidonia appears, however, he is hardly an exemplary idealist; he turns out to be a "dirty little old man" who demands payment for the bills which Bertie has contracted.

Trollope punctures all sentimental exaggerations. He gently mocks Victorian baby-worship when he renders Eleanor and Mary Bold's ecstatic chorus (" 'Diddle, diddle, diddle, diddle, dum, dum, dum: hasn't he got lovely legs?' said the rapturous mother. . . . 'H'm 'm 'm 'm 'm,' simmered the mama, burying her lips also in his fat round short legs."). He is less kind in exposing those distortions that stem from posturing and puffery. Throughout the novel, the signora invites her acquaintances to meet and comfort her fatherless child, the lonely descendant of the Neros and decadent remnant of a heroic race. Near the end of the novel, Mr. Thorne does see the little girl. She is dressed up extravagantly with a starched flouncy dress that spreads out horizontally from her hips: "It did not nearly cover her knees; but this was atoned by a loose pair of drawers which seemed made throughout of lace; then she had on pink little stockings." The squire is eager to make a favorable impression on the child's mother. Julia is thrust into his arms: "The lace and starch crumpled against his waistcoat and trowsers, the greasy, black curls hung upon his cheek, and one of the bracelet clasps scratched his ear." The bachelor gentleman, fifty years old, is somewhat at a loss; having, on other occasions, been compelled to fondle little nieces and nephews, he now sets about the task "in the mode he always had used":

> "Diddle, diddle, diddle, diddle," said he, putting the child on one knee, and working away with it as though he were turning a knife-grinder's wheel with his foot.
> "Mamma, mamma," said Julia crossly, "I don't want to be diddle diddled. Let me go, you naughty old man, you."
>
> (chap. 46)

Like Mr. Slope, this admirer must pay for his courtship of the exotic signora. The gallant squire finds himself in the uncomfortable position of a Humbert Humbert, denounced as a dirty old man by the Lolita he has bounced on his knees.

This kind of unmasking of the pretentious, the exaggerated, the oversentimental is one of Trollope's strengths. Though too gentle to be regarded as a satirist, he can effectively expose the human animal that lies behind the social mask. His aim is to strip men of their affectations, to divest them of all the gaudy untruths with which they try to conceal their share of universal imperfections. By openly exhibiting his own imperfections, Trollope's narrator constantly reminds the reader that most men and women are reducible to the same flaws. Their follies and foibles persist in any age. Although change and innovation provide Trollope with the stimulus for his comedy, this emphasis on persistence leads him to portray life as an uninterrupted and unvarying process. He prefers similarity to difference, permanence to fluctuation. His art thrives on what is durable and constant.

The history of the novel is one of change, of constant adaptation (the very name of the form connotes its capacities for perennial renovation). *Barchester Towers* appeared at a time when new social theories were burgeoning in England and when a new world picture began to threaten the cosmology accepted by Trollope's clergymen. Around this time, George Meredith and George Eliot were beginning their careers. Even earlier, other novelists had carried the novel beyond its eighteenth-century roots. Though starting in the tradition of Smollett and Fielding, Dickens had soon wandered into the hallucinatory realm of romance; the Brontës had published their own Gothic romances a decade before the appearance of *Barchester Towers.* What is more, *Vanity Fair* had been published in 1847. Trollope regarded himself as a kind of disciple of Thackeray's; in later life, he wrote an excellent study of the master. Like *Barchester Towers*, Thackeray's masterpiece relies on parody, burlesque, and satire; it too harks back to the mode of the eighteenth-century humorists. But Thackeray's novel displays the darker, more pessimistic vision that underlies so much of Victorian art: "It has to be confessed," wrote Trollope, "that Thackeray did allow his intellect to be too thoroughly saturated with the aspect of the ill side of things." In *Barchester Towers* Thackeray's disciple stoutly refused to yield to a capricious and changeful world; by allowing his intellect to defend itself through laughter he successfully resisted that "ill side of things."

The Warden and *Barchester Towers:* The Pastoral Defined

James R. Kincaid

These novels are about Mr. Harding and his enemies. They seek to tell us all about the two sides and the conduct of the battle, and they seek to convince us that Mr. Harding wins by losing. But really all that is finally necessary is to give us, as James said, "simply the history of an old man's conscience." Both novels are didactic portraits of Mr. Harding, complex in their means but quite single-minded in their ends. The ostensible issues matter very little in either novel, precisely because the morality advocated is aesthetic and intuitive rather than argumentative and rationalistic. *The Athenaeum* reviewer complained that *The Warden* showed "too much indifference as to the rights of the case," but "the rights of the case" are never a serious issue. In both novels the resemblance to the novel of ideas is very slight; they are both much closer to being modern saints' lives. Neither relies much on action to define that saint but rather depicts him by way of contrast and comparison with a series of more or less static portraits. Very near to Mr. Harding at the centre is the old Bishop, but he is dead as *Barchester Towers* gets under way, and there is no one but the Thornes to take his place. In the next circle is his daughter Eleanor, whose closeness to him is limited by her moral dullness; next is his other daughter Mrs. Grantly and, separated further, her husband the archdeacon. The archdeacon clearly moves closer to the centre in the second novel, but he is never really very far away. Beyond this there is a great gulf to the "new

From *The Novels of Anthony Trollope.* © 1977 by Oxford University Press.

men," the reformers: Slope, Mrs. Proudie, and John Bold. On the far edge is the voice of the *Jupiter,* most powerful and most destructive of all. Though it would appear from this that Mr. Harding is quite alone and though the novels do isolate him from other characters, the effect is less gloomy than it might be since, after all, he has the very close company of the reader.

In my view, it is a mistake, and a common one, to ignore the primary rhetorical purpose of these two novels and to read them in terms of some "reconciliation-of-opposites" theme. I do not believe that *The Warden* balances the views of Bold and the archdeacon or that *Barchester Towers* steers a course between past and future, conservative and liberal. Instead of the movement toward balance common to many other Trollope novels, *The Warden* and *Barchester Towers* describe patterns of disruption and consequent expulsion. Bold does not really have a "case," nor does Slope. It is not that their positions are bad but that they are irrelevant. Their assumptions about life and morality are so askew that they must be admitted only to be expelled. Both novels are subtle but quite unequivocal attempts to establish a positive and enduring moral centre. And they do so by running the reforming rascals out of town.

The Warden appears to have been begun with some spirit of reforming zeal. Trollope may well have initially thought of the novel in terms of the sort of satiric method he used in *The New Zealander,* written immediately after *The Warden,* and it may even be true that "for a moment, when he sketched out the plot of *The Warden,* Trollope half believed that he was on the side of the reformers" [as Knox writes in his introduction to the Barsetshire novels]. Trollope did speak of the novel later as if the satiric intention had got in the way of the moral intention, thinking that he was "altogether wrong" in supposing that he could attack the evil and also those who did the attacking (*Autobiography*). As far as the issues are involved, the novel does tend to do battle with both Bold and Grantly, but issues become trivial as the novel advances. It is almost as if Trollope discovered a new moral system on the way to writing a light topical satire. As this new intention takes over, the balance is upset completely, and the archdeacon is shifted as close to the centre as he well can be. The original intention makes the switch awkward, though, and the narrator is forced at the end to apologize for the picture of the archdeacon, saying that he is a much better man than he has been shown to be.

He is that, of course, according to the terms in which the novel ends. In fact, the only thing holding him from the centre is a certain coarseness that blinds him to the futility and danger of fighting for mere issues. But in its inception the novel imagined itself also to be interested in issues, and thus there are touches of materialism and hypocrisy added to the character: the copy of Rabelais, the narrative commentary which insists that he is "hard-hearted" (chap. 9), and a marital arrangement that anticipates the one later used with the Proudies. All this is a mistake, as the narrator is forced to admit. But it really does not matter a great deal in the end, since both Bold and Grantly are not so much opposing forces as flanking impotents who together teach Mr. Harding the proper moral position in respect to issues and conflict.

In terms of values, however, it is Bold's position, not the archdeacon's, that is dangerous. The archdeacon, however feeble his support, is on the side of the angels, and Bold, however well intentioned, serves the other side. Much of the apparent complexity of the novel comes from the narrator's charitable disengagement of Bold as a man from his position and the corresponding satiric disengagement of the archdeacon as a man from his office. As men, they are all good, if vain and fairly stupid. But this charity, which might be mistaken for equivocation, is certainly not applied to the moral issues. All men are to be treated gently but not all moral attitudes. Such an argument is, however, in itself a moral position. It is the position held by Mr. Harding but certainly not by John Bold and the *Jupiter,* who forget that there are individuals, who fail utterly to see interconnections between public and private life, and who treat morality as if it were a set of abstractions altogether divorced from human beings. There is no equivocation in the novel's point here; the humanistic and complex morality of Mr. Harding is attacked by an inhuman, simple, and abstract code. There is no question which side we are forced to join.

John Bold's decent position is decent only in the abstract, and when decency is thus abstracted it becomes nearly indecent. Failing to recognize for a long time the complex ties between men and morality, he becomes almost totally a public man, a terribly self-conscious reformer who teaches himself to live in the soft glow of clichés. He is able "to comfort himself in the warmth of his own virtue" (chap. 6), and he believes in the idiotic public response to him as the "upholder of the rights of the poor of Barchester" (chap. 2).

The narrator comments sarcastically, "I fear that he is too much imbued with the idea that he has a special mission for reforming. It would be well if one so young had a little more diffidence himself, and more trust in the honest purposes of others—if he could be brought to believe that old customs need not necessarily be evil, and that changes may possibly be dangerous" (chap. 2). The comparison to a "French Jacobin" (chap. 2) is pretty strong, as is Mr. Harding's "disgust" (chap. 3) at his ungentlemanly conduct. When Bold tells Eleanor that he has nothing against her father "personally," she asks, "Then why should he be persecuted?" Bold can only respond to this central question with "platitudes about public duty, which it is by no means worth while to repeat" (chap. 11). Bold's inability to understand the difference between Eleanor's feelings for her father and the hollow rhetoric of his own clichés is basic to the position he adopts. It does occur to him that the old men at Hiram's Hospital will only be hurt by his reforms—"to them it can only be an unmixed evil"— "but he quiets the suggestion within his breast with the high-sounding name of justice" (chap. 4). The great point made against his position is that it disrupts a happy situation and makes everyone unhappy. And for what? For the sake of platitudes. At the end, Bold does understand his error: "What is any public question but a conglomeration of private interests?" (chap. 15). He sees that a morality that separates public and private virtue is mad.

John Bold is not a bad man. He has, in fact, had the proper instincts all along. But he has been taught to "quiet them within his breast" by the great organ of the new insanity, the *Jupiter*. The *Jupiter* symbolizes this abstract morality with its frightening power: "What the Czar is in Russia, or the mob in America, that the *Jupiter* is in England" (chap. 7), says the archdeacon. The archdeacon allows the paper to stand for the alternate species of anarchy and dictatorship here, representing on one level his not very intelligent rage. There is, however, a point in the jumble, in that the *Jupiter* advocates with the single-minded simplicity of a tyrant the furious amorality of the mob. For public morality, the morality of abstractions and slogans, is no morality at all. It has no contact with people, just as Tom Towers, anonymous and out of reach, cannot be bothered to test his principles against human beings. His only morality, exactly like that of Slope, is a confident reliance on the virtue of his own elevation: "How could a successful man be in the wrong!" (chap. 15).

In a world like this, the only positive moral act is the act of withdrawal. Mr. Harding, "not so anxious to prove himself right, as to be so" (chap. 3), turns his back entirely on the doctrine of success. He sees that the law will not serve him—quite the contrary. Sir Abraham, his legal adviser, "conquered his enemies by their weakness rather than by his own strength" (chap. 8). Mr. Harding's resignation, therefore, is a radical affirmation, a refusal to live by a morality which crudely equates virtue with success and therefore disregards the private life altogether. He rejects proof of being in favour of being itself and thus affirms the primacy of conscience. The rejection of public morality does not imply a final isolation. It merely suggests that the abstract simplicities of public morality are threatening to overwhelm the intricate realities of personal conscience. Mr. Harding instinctively recognizes this and therefore declares war on the *Jupiter* by refusing to fight. His act is a moral one and asserts a connection between will and act, between the public and private life, that Tom Towers will never see. It is gloomy in the sense that it gives up external and obvious power altogether. It temporarily sacrifices appearances to the *Jupiter* in order to define and defend the integrity of the complete moral being. But then, appearances never counted for much anyhow.

In *Barchester Towers* appearances count for just as little. In fact, this novel really just fleshes out the shorthand sketch given in *The Warden,* largely by means of a much fuller description of the enemies and a wonderfully indirect defence of Mr. Harding. In a sense, it is *The Warden* turned into art. Having discovered a moral and aesthetic position, Trollope seeks in *Barchester Towers* to sanctify Mr. Harding by far more crafty means. The novel is surely a comedy, for instance, but it establishes itself as such while quietly subverting many of the major tenets of traditional comedy. It inverts the usual pattern of struggle between parents and children basic to all comedy and cheers very strongly for the parents, celebrating their escape from the young. Basic to the novel is its rejection of the values and assumptions of youth, as shown by the open sneers at babies and the often cynical impatience with the principal lovers. All this, of course, paves the way for us to travel to the moral crux of the novel, the sixty-four-year-old Mr. Harding.

Other comic principles are just as certainly and purposefully overturned. For example, comedy traditionally rests on an apprehension of man as a member of a social group and works to reestablish the harmony of society by eliminating or converting the individualists. *Barchester Towers,* however, directly reverses this assumption, seeing men as decent individually but dangerous, silly, or contemptible in so far as they define themselves as parts of a social organization. Similarly, comedy normally—the tradition is so firm that one almost says "naturally"—gives power to those who are approved: the good king is restored, the hero marries the girl, the money from the old will is accepted. In *Barchester Towers,* however, moral approval is directly proportionate to the decrease of power. More generally, comedy looks to the future and envisions a society cleansed and transformed by self-knowledge and joy. Most comedies deal principally with education and the resultant transcendence of the ordinary limitations of life; they are essentially progressive. Trollope's comedy, however, hates nothing so much as the callous notions of progress and sees forward movement as destruction. *Barchester Towers* looks to the past for its solidity and sees comic hope not in transformation but in preservation. Instead of seeking a transcendence of the ordinary, it revels in it. The most optimistic suggestion made by the novel is that the ordinary comforts of life are delicious, if only we perceive them fully and stop spoiling them by the continual anticipation of something better to come.

To establish this upside-down comedy, some extremely sly manœuvring is necessary. I have [elsewhere] indicated how the narrator's deceptive warmth urges us to adopt values which are gradually more and more specialized and which finally are contemptuous of the young. Many of Trollope's famous comments on novel-writing really have much the same thematic function. The narrator reflects at one point that if Eleanor had given way to her rising tears, Arabin would have declared his love, and the whole mystery would have been cleared up. "But then," he asks with mock ingenuousness, "where would have been my novel?" (chap. 30). Behind the companionable and easy rhetoric established by such an invitingly artless statement is a more quiet but more important attack on these almost-young lovers. Their actions are treated as mechanical, manipulable, and therefore trivial. The narrator takes them about as seriously as he expects the reader to, and the rhetoric here contributes to the irony which attends Mrs. Bold and Arabin throughout and which helps direct our moral concern to the elderly.

Though these passages do open the form of the novel, of course, they have a more particular thematic function. By attacking the very nature of form or pattern, particularly the whole notion of finality, they manifest a distrust for all neat patterns which point to the future. The narrator's position is that we must apprehend life as a continuous and organic movement, not as a fixed, forward-looking principle. His rhetoric brilliantly supports that very point and subtly directs our attention away from the conventional symbol of the time-bound Eleanor and Arabin, marrying, having children, and living happily ever after in power, and fixes it on the unconventional focus of the novel, the weak and retiring Mr. Harding.

Even more unconventional than the rhetoric, however, is the conservative comedy which is supported by the action and themes of the narrative itself. The organizing thematic principle in the novel is the notion of the fight. On all levels—clerical, academic, journalistic, and personal—the central issues involve a struggle for power. The book asks such questions as who shall be warden?—who shall be dean?—who will replace Mr. Bold with Eleanor? These and equivalent questions involving values are given one answer: he who does not try. The real winners are those who do not fight. At the heart of the book is a profound protest against the competitive mode of life, and *Barchester Towers* thus establishes its comedy in direct hostility to the major progressive movements of the period: democracy and capitalism. But the issue goes deeper than this; the whole notion of power is relentlessly attacked. It is power that unites the issues of religion and love in the novel and establishes the most basic irony in the plot, when the archenemies Grantly and Slope end up on the same side in the war over the wardenship. All the values of the conservative comedy here arrange themselves around the belief in passivity and its accompanying antagonism to ambition.

The novel begins, in fact, with a bleak view of power and a repetition of the distinctions developed in *The Warden* between man as a human being, personally defined and decent, and man as publicly defined, mad for power and dishonourable. Archdeacon Grantly's vigil at his father's deathbed brings into conflict the two sides of him, and though the question of "whether he really longed for his father's death" is finally answered with a clear negative, the archdeacon is not able to keep his desire for power completely under control. When his father finally dies, he itches to send his father-in-law to telegraph the ministry and is, appropriately, too late. The narrator ends the chapter by discussing the archdeacon's disappointment and his desire for power and position. As usual, he removes all personal censure and attacks only the system itself. Clergymen, he says, are, like all of us, only men, and "if we look to our clergymen to be more than men, we shall probably teach ourselves to think that they are less." Thus the first chapter effectively begins to assert the need both for tolerance toward individuals and hostility toward corrupting systems of power. Though as a worldly high-churchman the archdeacon is more obviously in accord with the principles valued by this novel, Trollope has an enormous amount of fun with this sputtering organization man, so eager for power and, in the end, so impotent: all his lectures go astray, all his plots come to nothing.

The attack on the alternate camp of churchmen is, however, the one that counts; for Mrs. Proudie and Mr. Slope are not only as much caught up in the lust of the fight as is the archdeacon but, in addition, are fighting for all the wrong values. Though the narrator introduces Mr. Slope (chap. 4) with an elaborate list of his similarities to Dr. Grantly, the implied differences are far more important. Where Dr. Grantly and the worldly high-church group assuage guilt, the Slopes and Proudies capitalize on it; Grantly is expansive and tolerant, while his enemies are restrictive and mean; Grantly is masculine, Slope, the most basic joke runs, is far less manly even than his comrade-in-arms, Mrs. Proudie. But no comparative listing can get close to the functional use made of the Proudies and Slope as negative illustrations to establish by contrast the novel's key position.

The Proudies are a symbol of local warfare and perverted ambition, and Trollope uses our laughter to attack both of them. Dr. Proudie, the epitome of the henpecked male, is still ludicrously ambitious and, sure enough, successful, all of which tells us something about the nature of success. He is known as a "useful" clergyman, a pawn of those who do indeed have power, particularly his wife. Mrs. Proudie is subject to some basic sexual humour and is a prototype of the big-bosomed, jewel-bedecked, pompous, and castrating females who are eternally attacked in literature. She reflects the novel's quiet but distinct antifeminism. By turning her into a kind of sexual amazon who, if all else fails, can still win her battles in the bedroom, Trollope appeals to sources of humour he so often claimed to have avoided. Slope, he says, might have had some chance in his fight with Mrs. Proudie had he been able to occupy her place at night. Since he cannot do this, Mrs. Proudie has, as we say, the ultimate weapon. These sorts of jokes transform both our tittering inhibitions and our sense of the grotesque into hostile laughter. Mrs. Proudie is besieged by other means too; she is not only rude but narrow, and no image is so firmly associated with her as that of the "Sabbath-day schools" and their suggestion of dreary, crushing repression. Mrs. Proudie is indeed the enemy of comedy as well as the perfect comic butt. The dominant joke against her is that she is simply a man; she is ranked with men rather than women, the narrator says with a nudge and a wink, because of "her great strength of mind" (chap. 33). There is more than a touch of the desperate in this sort of humorous attack, but by exaggerating the threat of conflict, it can call up laughter to eliminate that conflict and thereby suggest the positive values more clearly.

Compared with her chaplain, Mrs. Proudie is treated gently. It is the ambitious, progressive, and unctuous Slope who is the truly dangerous enemy and who is introduced so that the tendencies he represents may be expelled. In the process, he reveals a good deal about the moral premises of this comedy. The very fact that his eloquence is "not likely to be persuasive to men, but [is] powerful with the softer sex" (chap. 4), for instance, suggests that he is as feminine as Mrs. Proudie is masculine and uses a similar sexual humour to assault him. But more important, his specialized success suggests the fatal lack of discrimination of women in general and Eleanor in particular. Women, it turns out, are unable to see that he is "no gentleman," which, in terms of the code of *Barchester Towers*, means that they are morally cross-eyed. Slope's friends thus tell us nearly as much about him as his enemies. Eleanor is simply unable to understand her father when he gives the fundamental argument against Slope and, by implication, the central belief of the novel: "It can hardly be the duty of a young man rudely to assail the religious convictions of his elders in the church. Courtesy should have kept him silent, even if neither charity nor modesty could do so" (chap. 8). When Eleanor objects that he may simply have been forced by his inner convictions to speak, Mr. Harding replies, "Believe me, my child, that Christian ministers are never called on by God's word to insult the convictions, or even the prejudices of their brethren, and that religion is at any rate not less susceptible of urbane and courteous conduct among men than any other study which men may take up." The fact that courtesy and urbanity, rather than truth or righteousness, are the supreme moral touchstones gets us right to the heart of this novel. Eleanor's inability to comprehend this doctrine immediately distances her a little from the novel's centre.

But Slope's contributions are not often so indirect. He is the most vocal apostle of the new world, the oily symbol of progress, and the "new man" of the country: "It is not only in Barchester," he says, "that a new man is carrying out new measures and casting away the useless rubbish of past centuries. The same thing is going on throughout the country" (chap. 12). The "useless rubbish" in this case is Mr. Harding. The attack on Slope, then, is an attack on the *Jupiter* and all the rude voices of discourtesy. Once the chaplain leaves Barchester, the society can function comfortably enough with the Proudies, who, at any rate, have no such horrid convictions about useless rubbish. Slope has, all along, been the chief threat to comic equilibrium, and he has been granted no virtues. It is true, of course, that Trollope makes an elaborate show of treating Slope with a consistent and fair moderation, insisting on his great courage and self-sufficiency. But Slope's courage is of the brand more aptly described by the vulgar term "guts," and is thus completely out of place in a world of English decency. He has, in fact, exactly the characteristics of the ruthless and cunning animals who inhabit the America of *Martin Chuzzlewit*, and in many ways Trollope echoes Dickens's vituperative rejection of the new doctrine of "smartness" and the cult of success. Slope is a transplanted Colonel Scadder. The last reference to him makes his uncouth American newness even more explicit: "It is well known that the family of the Slopes never starve: they always fall on their feet, like cats" (chap. 51). What had been a matter of congratulation for Emerson in his strong celebration of the character of American youth, the "sturdy lad from New Hampshire or Vermont," who *"teams it, farms it, peddles"* and "always like a cat falls on his feet" (the famous passage occurs in "Self-Reliance"), becomes a matter of repulsion for Trollope in his equally strong rejection of it.

One of the major instruments of this rejection is the Stanhope family, fresh, lively, and not very scrupulous negative comic agents. Essentially foreigners, they not only have the clear insight of outsiders but the proper rootlessness and can act without final consequences to themselves. They do a job which the morally approved and passive cannot really handle. In their cynical and good-natured power, then, they add both the necessary purgative force and the rebellious parody to the valued innocence. As in most comedies, once their job is done, these negative agents must be dismissed; for their real work involves disruption, not stability. They also suggest an amusing but also dangerous lack of commitment. In combating the self-deluded Proudies and Slopes, their flexibility and manœuvrability are admirable, but, as Trollope insists, their very good nature hides an essential indifference, even heartlessness, and they must therefore be shipped back to Italy at the end. If we look at them too long, we might recognize their worldliness and laziness as parodies of the approved courtesy and passiveness. "I don't see why clergymen's sons should pay their debts more than other young men," says Charlotte (chap. 19). The cynicism is welcome and sounds very much like an echo of the narrator's insistence that we are all men, but the narrator really has a secret qualification, ignored by the Stanhopes. He suggests that we all are really gentlemen, pushing us upwards; the Stanhopes' cynicism levels downwards.

But Trollope handles these explosive agents with great tact. Their potential for danger is never realized, and their heartlessness is kept so well masked that they seem kindly, gentle, and, in the person of Bertie, essentially sweet. Bertie "was above, or rather below, all prejudices" (chap. 9) and is always absolutely comfortable in his friendly indolence. He functions partly to attack work, prudence, and rigid convention and is, therefore, something of a reverse surrogate for the author and is given a kind of sneaky admiration and approval. Absolutely without self-consciousness, Bertie is a natural man and, as such, a perfect comic leveller. He enters Mrs. Proudie's reception and immediately deflates the pompous bishop, attacking him just where he is most vulnerable—in his notion of the power bestowed by rank:

> "I once had thoughts of being a bishop, myself."
> "Had thoughts of being a bishop!" said Dr. Proudie, much amazed.
> "That is, a parson—a parson first, you know, and a bishop afterwards. If I had once begun, I'd have stuck to it. But, on the whole, I like the Church of Rome the best."
> The bishop could not discuss the point, so he remained silent.
> "Now, there's my father," continued Bertie; "he hasn't stuck to it. I fancy he didn't like saying the same thing over so often."
>
> (chap. 11)

Bertie continually pursues the bishop with his conversation, and his very amiability and openness—"I was a Jew once myself"—expose the pompous churchman. Significantly, though most of the clergy stare at Bertie "as though he were some unearthly apparition," "the archdeacon laughed." And that laugh carries with it the signal of moral approval for this fine comic executor. His climactic proposal (or antiproposal) scene, then, is carefully arranged to support the warm, uncommercial values. The narrator first makes it clear that Bertie is revolted by the "cold, calculating, cautious cunning" (chap. 42) of the affair, not so much because it is iniquitous as because it is "*prudent.*" He is the antithesis of the American-like Slope, instinctively repulsed by the game of power. In his gentle but firm rejection of the "new profession called matrimony" (chap. 42) he is rejecting all scheming, forward-looking arrangements. He is, in this sense, a heightened but not distorted symbol of the conservative tendency of the novel.

His sister Madeline plays a more complex role and brings with her a touch of a much blacker world and a more embittered spirit. However, she utilizes a kind of Freudian humour to transform her pain into clever parody and continual witty victories. Her calling card—"La Signora Madeline / Vesey Neroni./—Nata Stanhope"—is itself a fine parody of social forms, and she uses her daughter, "the last of the Neros," much as Becky Sharp uses little Rawdon, as an effective stage prop. Like her sister Charlotte, Madeline also sounds like the narrator: "Parsons, I suppose, are much the same as other men, if you strip them of their black coats" (chap. 10). Madeline's distance from that narrator is, however, clearly indicated by the violence of the verb "strip." Signora Neroni's function is potentially harsh, and she can, clearly, be vicious. She plays Sam Weller to Mr. Harding's Pickwick and supplies all the force and aggression he lacks.

She also provides a bitter realism, which adds force and depth to the final solution: "Marriage means tyranny on one side and deceit on the other. I say that a man is a fool to sacrifice his interests for such a bargain. A woman, too generally, has no other way of living" (chap. 15). Her cynicism is not explicitly supported, but since she does so much to ensure the solidity of the final approved society, the weight of her considerable experience and courage is assimilated into it. It is this crippled woman who is the most powerful. She manages not only to expose the hypocrisy and unprincipled ambition of Mr.

Slope and to force Arabin to recognize that the "good things of the world" are consonant with his religion (chap. 38) but actually hands him over to Eleanor, thereby arranging almost single-handedly the final disposition of the novel. The Signora Neroni has an absolutely sure moral instinct. Though she traps the virtuous Mr. Thorne and exposes the gentle old man and his "antediluvian grimaces and compliments which he had picked up from Sir Charles Grandison" (chap. 46) to some ridicule, she recognizes her error. And when Mr. Slope rudely laughs at him, she springs to the old man's defence, revealing the chaplain's failures with Mrs. Bold so ruthlessly that he dashes blindly from the room, while the avenged Mr. Thorne sits "laughing silently." She turns the tables on the powerful in this small scene as in the novel as a whole, adjusting the proper values and correcting our perspective. Because she is powerful, she cannot be made permanent in Barchester, but one suspects that she will be willing to come back from Italy should another Slope arrive. At any rate, she makes the cathedral town safe for the fragile values out of which the conservative comedy is built.

And all of the novel points toward the symbolic heart of this comic world and the structural centre of the novel in Miss Thorne's *fête-champêtre* at Ullathorne. The party, at first seen as a monstrous ritual of dedication to illusion and the dead, becomes the scene for clarity and rejuvenation, and the Thornes, viewed initially as hilariously superannuated, move closer to the approved position. The technique of diminishing perspective that Trollope uses here brings us closer to the Thornes and their values. Mr. Thorne is introduced in a tone of facetious detachment as a silly bore and a snob, supported by "an inward feeling of mystic superiority to those with whom he shared the common breath of outer life" (chap. 22). His sister, "a pure Druidess," simply exaggerates the fatuousness and obsolescence of her brother. The narrator's distance from these characters at first is so marked as sometimes to approach contempt: "Miss Thorne was very anxious to revert to the dogs" (chap. 22). We are encouraged to laugh at these unreal and mechanistic anachronisms. The only tonal variation in this introductory chapter involves a kind of nostalgic tolerance which is blatantly patronizing: "Who would deny her the luxury of her sighs, or the sweetness of her soft regrets!" The reader is led to view these people much as would Mr. Slope. But Trollope, even in this chapter, slyly exposes his method: "All her follies have, we believe, been told. Her virtues were too numerous to describe and not sufficiently interesting to deserve description." Her virtues are uninteresting only to the Slopes, and Trollope begins to reverse our position by forcing us much closer to the Thornes, quietly insisting in the next chapter on Miss Thorne's "soft heart" and essential good nature and on Mr. Thorne's honesty and generous hospitality.

By the time of the party, some ten chapters later, the Thornes' dedication to the past is taken much more seriously. They are rather like the Tudor windows at Ullathorne, not pleasing to utilitarian and modern progressive minds but capable of giving immense "happiness to mankind." Instead of measurable candle-power, the Thornes give comfort and joy. Exactly unlike Bold who, with laudable motives, made everyone miserable, the Thornes proceed with murky ideas to make everyone happy. Our earlier laughter is directly rebuked, as the Thornes' mechanistic unselfconsciousness is taken away and they are exposed as vulnerable and precious. In a fine scene just before the gathering, Miss Thorne tries to persuade her brother to ride at the quintain she has erected. Finally exasperated by the pressure she puts on him, he calls it a "rattletrap" (chap. 35). Miss Thorne says nothing, but sips her tea and thinks of the past. As she does so, "some dim faint idea of the impracticability of her own views flitted across her brain," and it occurs to her that "perhaps, after all, her neighbours were wiser than herself." The sadness of this moment of self-doubt brings a single tear to her eye, and Trollope uses that tear to establish the pervasive image of gentleness and kindness. "When Mr. Thorne saw the tear in her eye, he repented himself of his contemptuous expression." Miss Thorne, "accepting the apology in her heart," tells her steward to be very lenient in admitting guests: "If they live anywhere near, let them in." As it happens, they entertain nearly the entire district, and we see that the Thornes' deviation from the common standard, which had once seemed so funny, really amounts to their attempt to be truly kind and generous: "Miss Thorne . . . boldly attempted to leave the modern, beaten track and made a positive effort to entertain her guests" (chap. 36). Though she has only "moderate success," this reflects sadly on the times—not on the hostess. After Trollope has cemented our attachment to the Thornes by this rhetoric of reversal, we are easily led, later in the novel, to accept what would ordinarily appear perverse—the functional shift of love (and sexual power) from those who are young to the old Mr. Thorne: "But for real true love—love at first sight, love to devotion, love that robs a man of his sleep . . . we believe the best age is from forty-five to seventy; up to that, men are generally given to mere flirting" (chap. 37).

By this point the reader is also prepared to give full authority to Mr. Harding as the moral norm. The novel does include a pair of lovers, it is true, and does give them some prominence, but it seems to me an important critical error and a distortion of the crucial themes not to recognize the ironies which attend Eleanor and Mr. Arabin and the rhetorical instructions which move the reader away from them. It is particularly difficult to see how Eleanor can be accepted as a heroine. Not only is there a general distrust of women in the novel and a subtle but distinct antifeminine tone, but there are explicit attacks on the young widow. Eleanor, very simply, is morally stupid, and the dominant image connected with her is that of the parasite—clinging but deadly: "Hers was one of those feminine hearts which cling to a husband . . . with the perfect tenacity of ivy. As the parasite plant will follow even the defects of the trunk which it embraces, so did Eleanor cling to and love the very faults of her husband" (chap. 2). Again, when Arabin finally proposes, the narrator insists on Eleanor's prospective happiness in the same terms: "When the ivy has found its tower, when the delicate creeper has found its strong wall, we know how the parasite plants grow and prosper" (chap. 49). Even more subversive is the attack on Eleanor's selfish and sentimental use of her child: "It was so sweet to press the living toy to her breast and feel that a human being existed who did owe, and was to owe, everything to her" (chap. 2). Her essential lack of self-knowledge is exactly like that of Thackeray's Amelia Sedley and is mirrored in the same image of child-worship as a form of self-worship. Because of this ignorance Eleanor eagerly enters into the fighting, defending Slope often not from a sense of fairness but simply from instincts of "sheer opposition and determination not to succumb" (chap. 29). In the hilarious proposal scene with Mr. Slope, while we are expected fully to support the comic slap she gives him, we are also expected to delight in her embarrassment, the fruits of her ignorance. Both Eleanor's selfish reflections and Slope's champagne-induced "tender-pious" (chap. 40) looks are finally ridiculed; the scene really makes fun of the triviality of the young. After this buffeting at Ullathorne Trollope makes the criticism of Eleanor explicit. She rushes home to cuddle her boy and assert that she would die without "her own Johnny Bold to give her comfort" (chap. 44). The narrator cannot resist the appropriate sneer: "This kind of consolation from the world's deceit is very common. Mothers obtain it from their children, and men from their dogs. Some men even do so from their walking-sticks, which is just as rational."

While her eventual partner, Mr. Arabin, is not treated roughly, he is treated as more or less insignificant. Although not young, at forty he is not yet old enough to qualify for a favoured position in this novel. As a high-churchman most of his values can be approved, but he has dangerous ascetic tendencies and defends conflict for its own sake in terms which run exactly counter to the belief of the novel: "But are we not here to fight? Is not ours a church militant?" (chap. 21). Further, his adolescent stammerings and gapings in the presence of women are subject to a good many jokes (chap. 30). He is not a bad man, just an unimportant one. The narrator even laughs about having to mention the details of his engagement at all (chap. 48). In the end Mr. Arabin becomes a kind of Mr. Harding-in-training, committed to the old-fashioned and accepting from his father-in-law the deanship. Even at the last, however, Trollope throws out one final barb at this nearly irrelevant couple. Instead of promising eternal love and a proliferation of young Arabins, the narrator lets them repeat the marriage vows and cynically adds, "We have no doubt that they will keep their promises, the more especially as the Signora Neroni had left Barchester before the ceremony was performed" (chap. 53). This Dobbin and Amelia are certainly not allowed to dominate the novel.

But *Barchester Towers* is assuredly not "A Novel Without a Hero"; after virtually eliminating the standard interest in young love, the final focus rests on the true hero, Mr. Harding. While Mr. Harding's values are largely defined by negation, he does display, here as in *The Warden*, an immense strength of resistance, the true power of the pacifist. He demonstrates exactly those beatitudes which the narrator blames Mr. Slope's religion for slighting: "Blessed are the meek, for they shall inherit the earth—Blessed are the merciful, for they shall obtain mercy" (chap. 4). Mr. Harding "had nothing to seek and nothing to fear" (chap. 5), the narrator says, implying clearly that he can be unafraid *because* he has renounced the ludicrous power struggle. His withdrawing from conflict allows him a unique clarity and an important capacity for self-doubt ("not . . . the usual fault of his order" [chap. 7], the narrator sarcastically adds). His particular strength lies in his "nice appreciation of the feelings of others" (chap. 52). He alone has such clarity and generosity. While tolerant enough to allow "the Pope the loan of his pulpit" (chap. 7), as Dr. Grantly says in exasperation, Mr. Harding is neither soft nor naive. He immediately dislikes Slope for all the right reasons, and he firmly resists all the pressures put on him by his friends. His final triumph, then, reverses the general terms of comedy: his satisfaction, more complete than anyone else's (chap. 52), comes from declining power. In the world of fighting, Trollope argues, the man in the wrong is the one who is defensive, carefully storing up weapons, while the man in the right is confident and unarmed. "The one is never prepared for combat, the other is always ready. Therefore it is that in this world the man that is in the wrong almost invariably conquers the man that is in the right" (chap. 37). Hence, one does not fight. But in not fighting one preserves the moral life, a life which can be expanded again—once Slope leaves and the *Jupiter* quiets down.

The Boundaries of Barset

P. D. Edwards

It is a commonplace of criticism that Trollope failed to find his métier until the idea for Barchester came to him one evening during a stroll around Salisbury close. He was then in his late thirties. Previously, over a period of ten years, all he had produced were two Irish novels and a French historial romance. So *The Warden*, the first of the chronicles of Barset, marked his discovery not only of a new county but also of England itself. The point is worth noting because, although Barset has always been his best-loved and best-known creation, he was never content to withdraw into its boundaries completely. His next novel after *The Warden* and *Barchester Towers* was *The Three Clerks*, a novel of London life in which the world whose distant thunderings had occasioned such alarm in the cloisters of Barchester is the main arena. The next of the Barsetshire novels, *Doctor Thorne*, was followed, in *The Bertrams*, by another study of the sick hurry and divided aims of modern life, with the scene shifting restlessly all over England and half-way round the world. And even after *Framley Parsonage*, his first major success, Trollope continued to alternate between chronicles of Barset and kindred counties and novels dealing with the troubled mainstream of modern life.

The significance of this pattern of alternation is not as self-evident as it may appear. Obviously such a prolific author as

---

From *Anthony Trollope: His Art and Scope*. © 1977 by the University of Queensland Press.

Trollope could not restrict himself for long to one area, even one so congenial to him as the clerical and lay society of rural England. And however much his imagination may have hankered after rural fastnesses, his real-life pursuits and interests were clearly those of a townsman. But Barset had other limitations—for his imagination and his craft—which are perhaps less obvious and which do not apply at all to other rural counties. It was his own creature, his "dear county" (*Autobiography*); and it came to occupy a place in his affections and his scheme of values which no real-life setting could have filled.

Ostensibly, it is true, Barset almost is a real-life setting. In the very first paragraph of *The Warden* it is stated that Barchester, though not a real city, could have been any one of several: "Wells or Salisbury, Exeter, Hereford, or Gloucester." Readers during and since Trollope's own lifetime have pressed the claims of one city over those of another, and have also, on good grounds, added Winchester to the list of contenders. But whichever of these Barchester is most like, the important fact is that people have persisted in trying to identify it with places they know in real life. Many of the events that occur within it also invite comparison with well-known events in contemporary history. Early in *The Warden* we learn, for instance, that Archdeacon Grantly, the principal champion of inaction in the matter of reforming Hiram's Hospital, had taken a similar stand in the real-life case involving the St Cross Hospital at Winchester. He also has strong views on the scandal connected with the dismissal of Dr Whiston from the mastership of Rochester Grammar School. One case or the other is referred to no fewer than six times in the course of the novel. The object, one assumes, is partly to make it clear that the Hiram's Hospital case is not the Winchester or the Rochester case, and hence that the novel is not dealing in personalities; but at the same time the device serves to keep real-life analogues constantly in mind, so emphasizing the closeness of the novel's world to the real world.

A similar purpose is served by the reminders of contemporary history that are scattered throughout the Barsetshire series—and through the Palliser series which grew out of it. The period of most of the novels is precisely indicated, though on only one occasion— Frank Gresham's birthday in *Doctor Thorne*—is an actual date given to an event in the story. There is, moreover, a clear attempt to keep the chronology of the series as a whole more or less in step with historical chronology. *The Warden* is something of an exception in that the events it relates cannot be dated any later than 1847 or 1848, given the interval that is supposed to elapse between them and events in later novels; whereas the archdeacon's intervention in the Rochester case could hardly have occurred earlier than 1850. But in general the other Barsetshire novels are in accord, as regards both their internal chronology and their references to historical events, with the date given for Frank Gresham's twenty-first birthday, July 1, 1854. . . .

Even admitting that there are more inconsistencies of chronology than this account draws attention to, it is evident that the private lives related in the novels are placed in a very precise historical context, so much so that Barset almost demands to be squeezed into the history as well as the map of England. The gain in terms of realism—and, in some of the novels, of piquant topicality—is obvious. But these benefits sometimes entail disadvantages. In particular they tend to conflict with Trollope's growing attachment to Barset, his increasing reluctance to allow any real sway within its borders to the forces of social change that were at work outside. His attachment to it makes it something more than a replica of a real county with precise geographical and historical boundaries, a world that Meredith might have considered "over-real." From the beginning it has the air of an imaginative sanctuary, with a faintly mythic otherworldliness, and this becomes more pronounced in each new chronicle. Barset in fact evolves, showing in the process how deep and devious as well as how shallow and artless the stream of domestic realism in Trollope's novels can be. . . .

The Barchester that Trollope discovered on his evening stroll in Salisbury is a haven of traditional order under threat from new men and new ways. In its outward aspect it is the epitome of the "snug," the "picturesque." Some "scandals" it has already known, for instance the suspicion of nepotism in Mr Harding's appointment to a precentorship; but then it "scandalises" easily, as shown by its disapproval of Mr Harding's black neck-handkerchief. Of the major scandal about to break over it no more than "murmurs, very slight murmurs" have been heard. Ominously, however, the London road passes by the "ponderous gateway" that is so "unnecessary," but so "conducive to the good appearance" of Hiram's Hospital; ominously because it is from London that most of Barset's great upheavals come, including the one over Hiram's Hospital.

Confrontation between London and Barset runs right through the series. In *The Warden* it reaches one climax with John Bold's struggle against Tom Towers in the London office of the *Jupiter*: Bold, though styled "the Barchester reformer," is in fact half a Londoner and half a Barcastrian, but at this point he indignantly repudiates his alliance with the London radicals who had taken up his call for the reform of Hiram's Hospital. The most memorable climax comes, however, at the end of Mr Harding's "long day in London" dancing attendance on Sir Abraham Haphazard, the attorney-general (chap. 16). Here the utter strangeness of London in Mr Harding's eyes is conveyed by an account of his visit first to a cheap eating-house, then to a tawdry "cigar divan." It is a masterly piece of reportage, never far removed from stream of consciousness and eventually, by one of Trollope's most imaginative strokes, dissolving into surrealism as Mr Harding dozes off and, in a dream, his familiar images of Barchester become submerged in the vivid and baffling images of his last few hours in London.

Mr Harding's unsophistication is of course extreme even by Barchester standards, but he embodies in their purest form those traditional values for which Barset stands. In later novels these values sometimes find more formidable champions—Dr Thorne, Lady Lufton, and Mr Crawley—but only Mr Harding is absolutely pure in his motives. It is to him that Trollope returns at the close of *Barchester Towers*, in what amounts to an apology for the foibles and pettinesses of his other clerical characters:

> The Author now leaves him in the hands of his readers; not as a hero, not as a man to be admired and talked of, not as a man who should be toasted at public dinners and spoken of with conventional absurdity as a perfect divine, but as a good man without guile, believing humbly in the religion which he has striven to teach, and guided by the precepts which he has striven to learn.

No other character in any of Trollope's novels receives or merits such unequivocal praise; and certainly no other could lead even the "wordly" Archdeacon Grantly to question for a moment the whole basis of his own life:

> "The fact is, he never was wrong. He couldn't go wrong. He lacked guile, and he feared God,—and a man

who does both will never go far astray. I don't think he
ever coveted aught in his life,—except a new case for his
violoncello and somebody to listen to him when he played
it." Then the archdeacon got up, and walked about the
room in his enthusiasm; and, perhaps, as he walked some
thoughts as to the sterner ambition of his own life passed
through his mind. What things had he coveted? Had he
lacked guile? He told himself that he had feared God,—but
he was not sure that he was telling himself true even in
that.

(*The Last Chronicle of Barset*)

In this rare exalted moment the archdeacon can even credit Mr
Harding with having shown "all the spirit of a hero" in giving up his
wardenship of Hiram's Hospital. This, however, had not been his
opinion at the time, and if we can judge by the passage at the end of
Barchester Towers it had not been Trollope's either. "Had I written an
epic about clergymen," Trollope remarks at the end of *The Last
Chronicle*, "I would have taken St. Paul for my model," and in that
novel Mr Crawley actually does measure himself against Saint Paul.
But Harding is altogether too nervous and irresolute, and certainly
too modest, to be cast in such a role. In the archdeacon's view, he
cannot lay claim even to the less spectacular "heroism" that a man
may show in triumphing for a time over his weakness. For the
archdeacon still believes that Mr Harding's resignation, though
"right" for Mr Harding, would have been "wrong in any other
man" (*Last Chronicle*).

A corollary of the archdeacon's view must be that, however
right Mr Harding's motives, however consonant with his unworldly
purity, his resignation was a betrayal of the "right" cause, indeed a
betrayal of Barchester itself. If so, his position as the conscience of
Barset, the embodiment of its truest values, is seriously compro-
mised, perhaps even undermined. But judging from Trollope's
comments in his *Autobiography*, he didn't intend that the novel
should appear to endorse the archdeacon's view. Rather, Mr Harding's resignation was to be taken not only as a surrender—and
essentially an honourable surrender—to the reformers but also as a
gentle moral rebuke to the complacent self-interest of his own party,
led by the archdeacon. Trollope's stated aim was to draw attention to
"two opposite evils" that he had observed in recent controversies

about alleged misuse of charitable endowments. The "egregious malversation of charitable purposes" was of course one of these evils, but he wished also to stress the equally deplorable injustice which newspapers and others displayed in their "undeserved severity" towards the unwitting culprits. He accused himself, in retrospect, of an "absence of all art-judgment" in imagining that he could present both sides of the case, refusing to "take up one side and cling to that," and believed that, as a result, the novel had "failed altogether" in its "purport." The right weapons for dealing with such a controversial subject were not, as he had hoped, moderation and impartiality but satire and caricature.

If the novel does, as Trollope intended, remain neutral on the main points at issue between the reformers and the supporters of the status quo, then the moral satisfaction that accompanies Mr Harding's resignation is now shallow and delusory, as it must appear if he has mistaken his own motives, but the just reward for a right action. He is entitled to the sense of inner harmony and exalted moral vision that he displays in the scene where he forbids Sir Abraham Haphazard to take up the legal cudgels on his behalf:

> He was standing up, gallantly fronting Sir Abraham, and his right hand passed with bold and rapid sweeps before him, as though he were embracing some huge instrument, which allowed him to stand thus erect; and with the fingers of his left hand he stopped, with preternatural velocity, a multitude of strings, which ranged from the top of his collar to the bottom of the lappet of his coat. Sir Abraham listened and looked in wonder. As he had never before seen Mr. Harding, the meaning of these wild gesticulations was lost upon him; but he perceived that the gentleman who had a few minutes since been so subdued as to be unable to speak without hesitation, was now impassioned—nay, almost violent.

It is typical of Trollope to inject an ironic note—Sir Abraham's prosaic incomprehension—even into such a solemn moment as this; but there can be no doubt that he means us to take the purest of the arts, in this instance, as expressing the purest of moral sensations.

Yet in the novel as a whole some doubt does persist about the purity of these sensations. What if Mr Harding's sense of the real issues has as little substance as his imaginary cello? What if the imaginary cello is not a higher vision, but simply his cowardly refuge from reality? Such questions have been asked, and—misguided as they are—one can see why. The *Athenaeum*, for example, found the novel's conclusion—Mr Harding's resignation "lame and unsatisfactory," and accused Trollope of showing "too much indifference as to the rights of the case"; it complained of the "*laisser-faire, laisser-aller*" spirit of the book. Trollope perhaps took this sort of criticism as evidence of his want of "art-judgment" in failing to take sides between the reformers and the clerical party. But the *Eclectic Review* left no such room for misinterpretation, remarking that the novel lacks a "*moral*" because the impression it leaves is simply one of "regret at the affairs of the hospital having been brought into question." A similar complaint is implicit in Saintsbury's blunt assertion that Mr Harding is "nearly as much of a coward as of a conscientious martyr." Flying, as they do, in the face of Trollope's apparent intentions and Mr Harding's own estimation of his motives, these misjudgments can only derive from an impression, produced by the novel as a whole, that the evil to which Mr Harding appears to submit in resigning the wardenship is a good deal blacker than the evil he would be condoning if he retained it.

It is all too easy to see how such an impression might be produced. For while the novel is eloquent about the evil of vicious newspaper campaigns, sensational "reformatory" novels, and indiscriminate enthusiasm for change, it is surprisingly reticent about the opposite evil—the misuse of charitable funds—which the reformers have uncovered. Indeed, there is little evidence that this is an evil at all. We are very early reminded that "old customs need not necessarily be evil, and that changes may possibly be dangerous." We are also assured that whatever comes of the reformers' campaign it can only be an "unmixed evil" for Hiram's bedesmen themselves, who already have everything they need. And when the bedesmen decide to petition for a larger share of John Hiram's money, the narrator accuses them—with a perfectly straight face—of forming a "vile cabal" and displaying "deep ingratitude" to their warden. Considering that Mr Harding himself has defended their right to get up their petition, such strong language can only be taken as betraying the warmth of the narrator's own distaste for the methods of the reformers. Certainly, no comparable animus is shown towards the clerical party. At first the archdeacon is presented in an unfavourable light, presumably to place him more or less on a par with brash young John Bold: an unflattering picture is given of his family and of the chilly ostentatious luxury of his household (which may seem hard to square with his secret fondness for Rabelais); he berates the bedesmen in a manner which, the narrator concedes, is bound to arouse anger and disgust; and he rejects John Bold's penitent advances with brutal rudeness (chap. 12). Later, however, he softens marvellously, even to the extent of accepting the warden's decision to resign with barely a trace of rancour, and by the end we hardly need the novel's final plea for our forebearance: "We have seen only the weak side of the man, and have lacked the opportunity of bringing him forward on his strong ground." No such softening occurs in or towards any of his opponents—except John Bold, who changes sides.

Trollope's failure to strike a balance between his two "evils" is epitomized in his attack on the *Times* (the *Jupiter*), Carlyle (Dr Anticant), and Dickens (Mr Popular Sentiment). In this he not only drops any pretence of impartiality, or, as he had promised at the beginning of the novel, of avoiding "personalities," but resorts to the very weapons of satire and caricature that he is attacking and that he claimed to have dispensed with altogether in his own novel. The editor of the *Jupiter* for example, has to withstand this alliterative onslaught: "Quite true, thou greatest oracle of the middle of the nineteenth century, thou sententious proclaimer of the purity of the press—the public is defrauded when it is purposely misled. Poor public! how often is it misled! against what a world of fraud has it to contend!" Carlyle is pictured, in the same spirit of angry exaggeration, as "reprobating everything and everybody," and Dickens as specializing in "pattern peasants" and "immaculate manufacturing heroes" who "talk as much twaddle as one of Mrs. Ratcliffe's [*sic*] heroines." Such are the men who presume to teach Barchester its duty and to whose pressure Barchester, in the person of Mr Harding, is made to submit.

The cleverest and least exceptionable part of Trollope's attack on the real-life reformers is his parody of Dickens, which takes the form of a version of the Hiram's Hospital case as it might have been pictured in one of Dickens's novels. It shows an ugly, rapacious, port-besotted warden living in luxury on the money that should have been shared among the inmates of the hospital, while the inmates themselves, simple and saintly, are half-starved. Such a picture, the now repentant John Bold reflects, must be disqualified by its "absurdly strong colouring" from "doing either harm or good"; but the narrator disagrees:

> The artist who paints for the million must use glaring colours, as no one knew better than Mr. Sentiment when he described the inhabitants of his almshouse; and the radical reform which has now swept over such establishments has owed more to the twenty numbers of Mr. Sentiment's novel, than to all the true complaints which have escaped from the public for the last half century.

Here Trollope is in effect inviting us to contrast his way of writing a "novel with a purpose" with Dickens's, but he is also foreshadowing his admission of failure in the *Autobiography*, a failure that he attributed to his moderation in confining himself to "true complaints." Ironically, however, the chief weakness of *The Warden*, both as a novel with a purpose and as a work of art, is the very one that it was designed to expose and counteract. It is this weakness, as I have suggested, that blurs the significance of Mr Harding's fine moral gesture and in doing so compromises Barset itself in a way that Trollope clearly did not intend.

Michael Sadleir speaks of Trollope at this stage of his development and for several years afterwards as given to "tilting at windmills of contemporary abuse or misery" and "airing personal distaste for other folks' opinions." The prime example is his long journalistic jeremiad *The New Zealander*, which was written between *The Warden* and *Barchester Towers*; but *The Warden* also—as Sadleir implies—needs to be considered in the same connexion. Although its great achievement was the establishment, however uncertainly, of the Barchester ethos, it is generally different from the later Barsetshire chronicles. None of the others could seriously be considered as a "novel with a purpose" designed to contribute to a public debate; and in no other does Barset appear so vulnerable to outside influences, to sociohistorical processes beyond its control and emanating largely from beyond its borders. In the later novels Barset remains, as I have said, closely related to contemporary history, mirroring many of its changes; but at the same time it acquires a complexity and solidity of its own, and, with these, a resistance to, a power of excluding, aspects of contemporary life that it cannot comfortably assimilate.

The beginnings of this process can be seen in *Barchester Towers*.

Next to *The Warden*, this is the most obviously topical of the Barsetshire novels, the one that belongs most clearly to a particular moment of history: the immediate aftermath of the Oxford Movement and of the first period of church reform. It also resembles *The Warden*—more than any of the later novels—in that it consists, basically, of a series of confrontations between old Barchester and the outside world, the latter being represented most conspicuously by the low-church Bishop Proudie, his wife, and his chaplain Mr Slope, but also by the raffish, cosmopolitan family of Dr Stanhope, the high-and-dry prebendary. But although, as in *The Warden*, Barchester is only partially successful in its resistance to these alien influences, there is little of the bitterness that disfigures the earlier novel. *Barchester Towers* is, on the contrary, the gayest and most comically inventive of all Trollope's novels, the freest from that gloomy sense of "change and decay in all around" which is so marked in most of the other novels he wrote about this time. Barchester is still, as it had been in *The Warden*, one of the arenas of a fierce and nationwide debate, and this gives the novel a topicality that is a large part of its appeal even for the modern reader. But any views it may have as to the rights and wrongs or the likely outcome of this debate are incidental and well disguised: it could never be mistaken for a "party" novel, a "novel with a purpose," as contemporary critics—almost to a man, and from George Meredith down—noted with grateful relief. The old Barset is now much surer of itself and of its ability to wage an equal struggle with the forces of historical change; and Trollope's delight in the comic relish that both sides show for the struggle, the vitality and resourcefulness that they bring to it, carries far stronger conviction than his "true complaints" about the existence of such struggles.

It is in *Barchester Towers* and *Doctor Thorne*, the next novel in the series, that the struggle is fiercest and most exciting; in *Framley Parsonage* it becomes narrower in scope and less momentous, in *The Small House at Allington* it stiffens into deadlock, and by *The Last Chronicle* it is effectively over. One result of this progression is that the earlier novels, *The Warden, Barchester Towers,* and *Doctor Thorne*, appear more tightly constructed than the later ones: they have a definite animating idea; they are, relatively speaking, "well-made books" with the advantages that derive from a degree of compression and concentration. But more important they also have an imaginative freshness, a dynamic, a sense of direction, which are lacking in many of Trollope's other essays in domestic realism.

Barchester Towers, it is true, is not usually thought of as a well-made and dynamic book. Laborious Homeric similes, and thee-thouing authorial addresses to the reader and even to the characters, are more frequent than in most of the later, "mature" novels. Caricature and slapstick, styles of humour that don't usually suit Trollope, are more prominent than in most of his best work. And the love-plot is among his most protracted and dull. *Barchester Towers* is also supposed, wrongly I believe, to be unusually discursive even for Trollope, the episodes connected with Mr and Miss Thorne coming in for special condemnation on this score. All these elements, however, seem to me conditions of the novel's strength, which consists above all in the finely sustained note of informality, mocking and self-mocking, that disguises both its sharpness of focus and its deep emotional commitment to the world it describes.

Seen in this light, it is much less artless than it pretends to be and is often taken to be. A case in point is the seemingly heavy-handed use of the "authorial I," to which James in particular took exception. In *Barchester Towers* Trollope intrudes into the novel not only in order to pass judgment on or admonish his characters, or to appeal to us to share his own feelings about them, but also at times to mock the whole ritual of narration. When he chips in to reassure us, well in advance of the event, that Eleanor Bold will certainly reject both Mr Slope and Bertie Stanhope, he is merely exercising the narrator's privilege of breaking with strict chronological sequence, and he is doing so on respectable grounds—to put pointless speculations out of court. However, when he asks, by way of explaining Eleanor's failure to display the womanly tenderness that would have averted a misunderstanding between her and Mr Arabin, "But then where would have been my novel?"; and when he pronounces that the "end of the novel, like the end of a children's dinner-party, must be made up of sweetmeats and sugar-plums," he may well seem, as James complains, to be delivering "slaps at credulity" and reminding us that the story is "only, after all, make-believe." But in fact he is not admitting that he has invented the story—which is what James accuses him of doing; all he is saying is that he has chosen a story, perhaps from life, that has the ingredients a conventional reader is likely to expect. The effect, then, is not necessarily harmful to the realistic illusion that the novel as a whole clearly aims at, though no doubt it may induce us to take some things—such as the manner in which the love-plot strings itself out—less seriously, with more of a feeling of déjà vu, than others. It may also, and this I think is of more consequence, accustom us to the idea that a good deal that happens in the novel is every bit as strange as fiction, but is not, for that reason, to be taken less seriously or as less true to life.

For *Barchester Towers* probably contains more to tax the credulity of the prosaic mind than any of Trollope's other "domestic" novels. Some of the characters are obviously caricatured, Mr Slope being only the most notorious example; farce and slapstick are used with memorable effect in many scenes, notably in those of Mrs Proudie's reception (chaps. 10–11) and Mr Slope's "parting interview" with the signora (chap. 46); and there is a flavour almost of fantasy in the story of the signora's marriage and in the description of the Thornes (chap. 22). Yet at the same time, as I have suggested, the novel is very closely related to contemporary history, and it offers not only what seem like highly realistic details of the customs, manners, and preoccupations of particular social groups at a particular point of time, but also, for example in the biographical sketch of Mr Arabin (chap. 20), a realism that can only be described as documentary. The art and imagination that assimilate all these elements into a unity—or a close approximation to one—hardly deserve to be called immature.

What is most impressive about the novel's formal and imaginative unity is the number of contrasting perspectives it accommodates. These have the effect, primarily, of keeping us in constant doubt as to the reality, if any, that underlies the ostensible values of Barset. The crucial question in this regard is very much the same as in *The Warden*: whether in human and in objective ethical terms there is anything to choose between the old Barset and the new and foreign ways that threaten it. But much more than in *The Warden*, the elusiveness of old Barset's own special qualities is acknowledged. In *The Warden*, it will be recalled, the repetition of the word picturesque seemed to provide an essential clue, but the picturesqueness of Mr Harding's position was not sufficient to allay his doubts about its ethical correctness. In *Barchester Towers*, however, the epithet that catches our attention at the outset is *worldly*. It is applied to the archdeacon no fewer than three times in chapter 1, and on the last occasion is accompanied by what amounts to an authorial manifesto: "Our archdeacon was worldly—who among us is not so?" This is but the first of many reminders that the clergyman, like any other professional man, is worthy of his hire and not usually backward, however exemplary his piety, in claiming it. The idea is one of the novel's great comic themes, and indeed becomes for Trollope an inexhaustible mine. And although Mr Harding and his liturgical music still haunt the cloisters, although in the chapter called "The Rubbish Cart" there is a further cry of petulant nostalgia for the good old days, quite in the manner of *The Warden* at its worst ("New men and new measures, long credit and few scruples, great success or wonderful ruin, such are now the tastes of Englishmen who know how to live"), worldliness has clearly become the dominant spirit even of old Barset. Picturesqueness, moreover, is now personified not only by Mr Harding but more vividly by the Thornes of Ullathorne, in whom it is shown running to delightful but bizarre excess.

The Thornes (and, in a less likable way, the De Courcys) represent Barset in its "feudal" aspect, about which Trollope waxes so lyrical in *Doctor Thorne*. But the Thornes also reflect, in a distorting mirror, many aspects of Archdeacon Grantly and his worldly colleagues. For the archdeacon's seemingly prosaic worldliness includes at least a dash of poetry, as Trollope implies when he observes that it is not to be mistaken for mere "love of lucre": "He would be a richer man as archdeacon than he could be as bishop. But he certainly did desire to play first fiddle; he did desire to sit in full lawn sleeves among the peers of the realm; and he did desire, if the truth must out, to be called 'My Lord' by his reverend brethren." Of his three main reasons for wishing to be a bishop, we note that two relate rather to the picturesque emblems of the office than to the actual power and worldly advantage it might confer. And it is noteworthy too that right through the novel he is cast in the role of defender of picturesque anomalies—of the "meretricious charms of melody" in cathedral services, though he will not tolerate "intoning" in his own church; of a wardenship with virtually no duties but a high salary and comfortable house attached to it; and of a deanship that carries great authority and status but virtually no duties (" 'New duties! what duties?' said the archdeacon, with unintended sarcasm. . . . 'And where on earth can a man have peace and rest if not in a deanery?' "). The archdeacon and his friends, we are told, are "all of the high-and-dry church," and in many of their attitudes they appear scarcely less high and dry than Miss Thorne and her brother—Miss Thorne who is a "pure Druidess" in her passion for the past, and Mr Thorne for whom Peel's "apostasy" on the question of free trade meant that "politics in England, as a pursuit for gentlemen, must be at an end," and whose heroes are "those fifty-three Trojans" who brought down the Whig-Peelite government in November 1852.

Yet the dominant feeling that the picturesque side of Barchester's highness and dryness leaves with us is one of incongruity. For in its most characteristic manifestations the spirit of old Barchester is nothing if not practical and contemporary. This is brought home to us in the early scene where the archdeacon, at the bedside of his dying father, lays his plans for ensuring that he will succeed him as bishop. It is also dramatized in the anxious chatter of the clergymen gathered outside the room where Dean Trefoil lies dying. Here solemn, but conventionally parsonical, solicitude for the sick man struggles with an in every sense livelier solicitude about who will be the next dean. The archdeacon is shocked by such discussion at this time, but even he turns pale and quite forgets Dr Trefoil when a "meagre little prebendary" mentions Mr Slope as a possible successor. A tersely businesslike argument about stipends and reports then follows. And although the impression of worldliness is softened by the clergymen's touching confusion about the facts which matter so much to them, and ironically punctuated by the choric repetition of the quaint titles which are their sole identifying marks, their prosaic absorption in questions of preferment and money must be judged unseemly.

In human terms, of course, these men are decidedly more agreeable than their low-church adversaries. They don't smell, or exude grease, like Mr Slope; they aren't rigorous about Sunday observance; they remember with pleasure a time when, without provoking censure, parsons played cards and hunted and enjoyed their wine like other gentlemen, and when, as Mr Harding recalls with some contrition, they were sometimes "very idle" (*Last Chronicle*); they are not, in ordinary circumstances, aggressive or impolite in propagating their own tenets. Trollope, in the novel, makes no secret of his liking for them, nor, though he tries to be casual about it ("My readers will guess from what I have written that I myself do not like Mr Slope; but I am constrained to admit that he is a man of parts"), of his loathing for the worst of their enemies.

But on balance—in *Barchester Towers* if not always in other novels—Trollope recognizes that whatever his personal feelings, the high and dry cannot be represented as markedly more altruistic or morally aware, and certainly not as more truly religious, than the low. Even Mr Slope has taught himself, by "that subtle, selfish, ambiguous sophistry to which the minds of all men are so subject," to believe that "in doing much for the promotion of his own interests he was doing much also for the promotion of religion." In any case, Mr Slope finally discredits himself even with his own party, so that we may take it that his grossest exhibitions of greed and duplicity place him outside the low-church pale. As to his lesser faults, the gist of the indictment seems to be that he is not a gentleman, as all of the high and dry unmistakably are. The archdeacon snarls that he has been "raked up . . . from the gutters of Marylebone"; but this, we must remember, is after Slope has affronted the archdeacon by seeming to hold him personally accountable for the inadequacies of the plumbing and other amenities of the bishop's palace. (Ironically, we later find that the archdeacon is not above interesting himself in such matters after all, for he looks into the domestic arrangements at Mr Arabin's parsonage with housewifely minuteness.) Despite the fact that Slope had been at Cambridge—though only as a sizar—the archdeacon's doubts about his social status may be justified. Not even the archdeacon, however, would deny that Bishop Proudie is a gentleman; and when in a moment of fury he unconsciously degrades the bishop to the same level as the bishop's chaplain, the laugh is clearly against the archdeacon himself:

> "He is the most thoroughly bestial creature that ever I set my eyes upon," said the archdeacon.
> "Who—the bishop?" asked the other, innocently.
> "Bishop! no—I'm not talking about the bishop. How on earth such a creature got ordained!—they'll ordain anybody now, I know; but he's been in the church these ten years; and they used to be a little careful ten years ago."
> "Oh! you mean Mr Slope."

The archdeacon's wildness here is only one of many indications that high-and-dry Barchester is neither more reasonable nor always more gentlemanly in its prejudices than are its enemies. Indeed there are innumerable hints that both sides are tarred with much the same brush. Petticoat government, for example, may seem the special bane of the low-church party, but it is not unknown, either, in the household of the archdeacon himself: he finds himself badgered by his wife to put a stop to Mr Arabin's flirtation with the signora just as the bishop is badgered by Mrs Proudie about Mr Slope's association with the same lady; and we observe, too, that it is the archdeacon's wife, not the archdeacon himself, who drops the few discreet words that silence the "intoning" curate of Plumstead Episcopi. In a more general way, attitudes to women, and the behaviour expected of them, represent an important bond between the two parties. If Barchester is united in any respect, it is in its mingled cruelty and vulnerability to women. The signora highlights the vulnerability because she can exploit, and brilliantly expose, a situation in which there is a universal assumption that unattached woman is the weaker vessel, both intellectually and morally. In the eyes of the men, the outrageous promiscuity of the signora's flirtations (with Arabin as well as Slope, Mr Thorne as well as the bishop) is the sign of an essentially feminine weakness and dependence, too flattering to themselves not to be readily forgiven and enjoyed. But when the same male superstition convicts Eleanor Bold, unheard, of being infatuated with Slope, she is cruelly ostracized because she refuses to simulate feminine weakness. So long as she takes her stand on rational moral grounds—arguing that Slope need not be her enemy simply because he is of the low-church party—she is misunderstood. And eventually, though it has been maintained that she achieves some degree of heightened self-knowledge, she is driven, as I see it, to the same abject surrender, the same admission of weakness, as nearly all of Trollope's heroines who try to assert their own judgment on matters outside the domestic sphere.

Admittedly, Eleanor's marriage to Arabin may appear, and may be meant to appear, a marriage of true minds. Arabin is ostensibly the most serious and least rancorous of the high-church party, and he alone seems to see the Barchester struggle in something like its correct perspective. "Wars about trifles," he points out, "are always bitter, especially among neighbours." But he will not have it that "such contentions bring scandal on the church." The only alternative to them would be "that of acknowledging a common head of our church, whose word on all points of doctrine shall be authoritative." Having nearly followed Newman into the Roman church, he is aware that "such a termination of our difficulties is alluring enough." But in the existing situation his view clearly coincides with that already expressed by the narrator:

> Moderate schism, if there may be such a thing, at any rate
> calls attention to the subject, draws in supporters who
> would otherwise have been inattentive to the matter, and
> teaches men to think upon religion. How great an amount
> of good of this description has followed that movement in
> the Church of England which commenced with the pub-
> lication of Froude's Remains!

On the evidence of the novels, one may wonder whether Trollope's
sense of this "good" was really as strong as he suggests here. But
Eleanor, at any rate, hears Arabin's ideas "not without a certain
pleasurable excitement, that this new comer among them spoke in a
manner very different from that to which she was accustomed." It is
a surprise to her to learn that there is a spiritual dimension to the
disputes that she has seen raging about her and that at least one of the
participants can admit that neither side has a monopoly of the truth.
Yet it does not appear to shock either her or Trollope that Arabin
should share and vociferate the general eager dislike of Slope, even
before he has met the man!

Neither Eleanor nor Arabin, then, attains to anything like
complete detachment from the fray. For this, and for the sense of
how little there is to choose, objectively, between the contending
parties, it is to the Stanhopes—particularly Bertie Stanhope and his
sister the signora—that we must turn. These are the jesters, whose
function is to expose the common denominator of humanity that is
overlaid by distinctions of rank, opinion, and deportment. Their
great qualification for the role is not their ethical sense—for they are
all "heartless" and all, in varying degrees, unscrupulous—but their
complete aloofness and disinterestedness, their impervious bland-
ness. They are, in fact, the only absolute outsiders ever allowed into
Barset, and after they leave it never recovers the same animation or
has its lovable and unlovable absurdities exposed with the same
sharpness and joy. Subsequently, I suggest, Trollope became too
attached to the county—just as, for example, he became attached to
the archdeacon during the course of *The Warden*—to feel comfortable
with observers so unattached, so oblivious of its traditional values.
But it may also be that he took to heart the suggestion of his
publisher's reader that the signora in particular might shock the
Young Person, and the emphasis of friends and reviewers on the
book's "manliness." It is, at all events, unhappily true that none of

his later novels—not even *The Eustace Diamonds*—can compare with *Barchester Towers* for gleeful irreverence, especially on the subjects of sex and religion. "Is it not a pity," he asks at one stage, "that people who are bright and clever should so often be exceedingly improper? and that those who are never improper should so often be dull and heavy?" But too often in his later novels, and especially those in his domestic stream, we sigh in vain for improper people who are also bright and clever.

The impact of the Stanhopes on Barchester, and on our view of Barchester, is seen at its strongest in three scenes: Mrs Proudie's reception (chaps. 10–11), the confrontation of the signora, Lady De Courcy, and Mrs Proudie at the Ullathorne sports (chap. 37), and the signora's humiliation of Mr Slope (chap. 46).

At Mrs Proudie's reception, Bertie's unintentional chaffing of the bishop is not only funny in itself—because of the bishop's discomfiture and Bertie's obliviousness of it—but also very pointed as a commentary on the temporal preoccupations of the Barchester clergy generally. Bertie assumes unquestioningly that one addresses a bishop as man to man: "Bishop of Barchester, I presume? I am delighted to make your acquaintance." Instinctively polite, he easily finds common ground between them: "Do you like Barchester on the whole?" he asks, recalling that the bishop is as much a stranger in Barchester as he is. The next question, naturally, is how the bishop likes his new job and whether it is a promotion or just a transfer:

> "You are changed about sometimes, a'nt you?"
> "Translations are occasionally made," said Dr. Proudie;
> "but not so frequently as in former days."
> "They've cut them all down to pretty nearly the same
> figure, haven't they?" said Bertie.

"They," in this connexion, are presumably the bishop's own Whig friends and patrons, but the real sting is less in Bertie's casual way of referring to the church reforms that have meant so much to the bishop and, in a more distressing way, to Barchester, than in the implication that a bishopric nowadays is not a very lucrative or even a very dignified position: the word *figure* must strike the bishop as cruelly double meaning. Perhaps, however, there is not much for a bishop to do at Barchester? Bertie's query foreshadows the archdeacon's scornful mirth at the idea that deans have duties. The bishop replies, "with considerable dignity," that a bishop of the Church of England never has an easy lot. Bertie confesses that he "once had thoughts of being a bishop" himself, or rather, he corrects himself, "a parson first, you know." What put him off, he remarks with crushing but still quite unconscious irony, was not the prospect of hard work—though he admits that his father has found it too much ("I fancy he didn't like saying the same thing over so often")—but his preference for the Church of Rome and more recently for the Jews. Here Bertie, and not Arabin, stands forth as the prime representative in the novel of contemporary religious unrest. And one cannot help wondering whether he is not a better guide than Arabin to Trollope's own attitude to this unrest. For Trollope at times seems to find as much to respect in Bertie, with his harebrained involuntary parodies of clerical attitudes, as he does in any of the clergy, and the tone of some of his references to the clergy in general, while inoffensive enough, is a good deal more flippant than he usually allows it to become. The "preaching clergyman," for instance, is characterized as "the bore of the age," and it is suggested that, if deacons were prohibited from preaching as well as from pronouncing absolution, they would never be allowed by their congregations to advance to full priesthood but would be "bribed to adhere to their incompetence."

Bertie's exchange with the bishop is followed by the near-slapstick incident in which Mrs Proudie's lace train is damaged by the castors of a rolling sofa, probably the very sofa from which Mrs Proudie herself is wont to preside in the bishop's study and which, it has been suggested before, is a fitting emblem of the new regime at the bishop's palace: "a horrid chintz affair, most unprelatical and almost irreligious: such a sofa as never yet stood in the study of any decent high church clergyman of the church of England." It is now the throne of the crippled signora, conspicuous under the blazing gas lamps that are another of the Proudies' innovations at the palace. As the substructure of Mrs Proudie's train begins to tear, and crack, and gape open under the assault of the sofa, every detail in the mélée that follows is beautifully calculated: Bertie's involuntary homage to Mrs Proudie as an enraged goddess; Mrs Proudie's misconstruction of Bertie's poetic promise to "fly to the looms of the fairies to repair the damage [to her lace]" as a "direct mockery" of her; the manner in which "Bertie" becomes "Ethelbert" as he attempts to respond to Mrs Proudie's "Unhand it" (opportunely recalled from some "scrap of dramatic poetry") with something equally poetic; the collocation of Bertie's blasphemous reference to the "cursed sofa" with the devotionally "imploring" face he turns to Mrs Proudie; the suggestive vagueness of the word *belongings* as applied to Mrs Proudie's nether garments; and the telling redundancy of the signora's "audible" laugh. In real life the niece of an earl, albeit a "Scotch" earl, would not say "Unhand me," or would say it more effectively; but incredulity gives way to sheer delight at the stylized eloquence of the scene.

The importance of Bertie's and Mrs Proudie's contretemps for the novel as a whole lies in its sexual overtones. Bertie and Mrs Proudie are clearly terrified of each other, Bertie because Mrs Proudie's stateliness unmans him, accentuates his usual effeminacy ("I'll fly to the looms of the fairies"), Mrs Proudie because she feels, no doubt unconsciously, in danger of a sexual assault. The irony of Mrs Proudie's fear is that here as always—as, for example, in her usurpation of her husband's prerogatives both in the home and in the diocese—she is playing the man's part and would be in little danger of losing her dignity but for this. The signora, who specializes in humiliating men, and who succeeds in making not only Slope and the bishop but also, on the other side, Arabin and Mr Thorne look foolish, probably senses that her effeminate brother is unconsciously using tactics very like her own—a "poetic" affectation of weakness—to humiliate the mannish Mrs Proudie. Of Charlotte Stanhope, Bertie's other sister, the narrator observes that she "was a fine young woman; and had she been a man, would have been a very fine young man," and the same, with minor variations, could be said of Mrs Proudie. Both of them, like the signora herself, and to some extent like Mrs Grantly and even Miss Thorne (with her passion for muscular medieval sports), are natural man-tamers. Bertie, however, though Charlotte likes to feel she has him under her domination, nearly always wriggles out, obeying her according to the letter—for example, by proposing to Eleanor—but resisting her according to the spirit. He is, in fact, the sole exception to the male pomposity which, as I have noted, makes so much misery for Eleanor, and which, chiefly as a result of the wiles of the signora—reaching their climax in chapter 46 with her dressing down of Mr Slope—we come to see as a crucial weakness that the old Barchester shares with its enemies.

Why did Trollope choose to make the signora a cripple? One's first impulse is to say that he was simply playing safe: a sexually incapacitated siren would not compromise her male admirers to the same extent as one they could be suspected of hoping to seduce. But is it credible that she could have cast such a spell over so many men? The realistic answer must be no. But if we consider it as another of those elements in the novel which border on comic fantasy, the signora's remarkable seductiveness can be seen to serve a distinct satirical purpose: that of showing up the sexual timidity of the Barcastrian, and perhaps the Victorian, male. In *The Ordeal of Richard Feverel*, published two years after *Barchester Towers*, Adrian Harley mockingly observed that unless he happened to go to the ballet a Victorian young man might well remain ignorant of the fact that women possess legs; and it is presumably this comforting ignorance that beguiles the signora's male coterie. What is certain, however, is that her sexual incapacity is one of the conditions of her emancipation from conventional standards, just as her brother's effeminacy is one of the conditions of his; and it is by contrast with this emancipation that the timidities of Barchester appear most absurd.

The signora's satirical gaze of course takes in more than the sexual quirks of Barchester. She is also fully alive to the absurdities of its caste system, of which we are given a not altogether farcical parody in the imbroglio over the "classless" Lookalofts at Miss Thorne's fête. It is, for example, her amused awareness that Mr Slope is not the stuff of which Barchester deans are made that gives her such an advantage over him in the scene where she publicly ridicules him. And she can use her own patently apocryphal claim to exalted rank—as the "last of the Neros"—with a perfect simulation of innocence: for example, when she sets out to embarrass the bishop by seeming to hint that he might personally prepare her daughter for confirmation. But her greatest moment is when she outstares the Countess De Courcy:

> She opened her large bright lustrous eyes wider and wider, till she seemed to be all eyes. She gazed up into the lady's face, not as though she did it with an effort, but as if she delighted in doing it. She used no glass to assist her effrontery, and needed none. The faintest possible smile of derision played round her mouth, and her nostrils were slightly dilated, as if in sure anticipation of her triumph. And it was sure. The Countess De Courcy, in spite of her

thirty centuries and De Courcy Castle, and the fact that Lord De Courcy was grand master of the ponies to the Prince of Wales, had not a chance with her. At first the little circlet of gold wavered in the countess's hand, then the hand shook, then the circlet fell, the countess's head tossed itself into the air, and the countess's feet shambled out to the lawn. She did not however go so fast but what she heard the signora's voice, asking—

"Who on earth is that woman, Mr. Slope?"

"That is Lady De Courcy."

"Oh, ah, I might have supposed so. Ha, ha, ha. Well, that's as good as a play."

This is a scene that Trollope often attempts but never does so well again. But then, except perhaps in one of his last novels, *Mr. Scarborough's Family*, he never again allows himself to portray such an emancipated spirit as that of the Stanhopes with the same imaginative freedom.

Certainly, Barset is never afterwards exposed to quite so unblinking a gaze. At the end of *Barchester Towers* the Stanhopes return to Italy, where, it is reported in *Doctor Thorne*, Dr Stanhope soon after dies (though in *Framley Parsonage* he is reported to have come back and lived at Barchester before his death). Slope also departs, and with Arabin ensconced in the deanship the old Barchester is left to carry on its struggle with the Proudies on equal, if not advantageous, terms and in no further doubt as to its own survival. In the later Barsetshire chronicles, even when clerical characters play a major part, the struggle becomes essentially social and political, with religious, or at any rate sectarian, issues receding into the background.

Trollope's *Barchester Towers:* Comic Reformation

Robert M. Polhemus

> *Institutions establish the community of men: a "church" means that many men have had an idea of goodness, but it is part of that goodness to perpetually need to be rediscovered and reestablished in the flux of history and of changing, "reforming" society, in each individual situation.*
> RUTH APROBERTS

Trollope's *Barchester Towers* is at the heart of the great comic tradition. It brings together religion and comedy and implicitly juxtaposes prayer and laughter. The most obvious thing about the novel is also the most important: the ecclesiastical establishment is made the subject of comedy, and Trollope's imagination establishes a comic church. The allegiance of Barchester's religious institution and its members has quietly passed from God to humanity, but its corporate structure remains, and Trollope respects it.

His humor, however, dissolves the aura of divinity around the church, and no matter how he might wish to deny it, the logical drift of this book implies that nothing, theoretically, is sacred—nothing, that is, is beyond comic scrutiny. Though there is no direct scoffing at the church and little that a confirmed Anglican could resent, the novel is in the broadest sense irreverent. It makes theological presumption seem ridiculous. What religious feeling there is resides not in "orthodox Christian supernaturalism" but in Trollope's comic vision of life. He values, and projects fictively, community,

From *Comic Faith: The Great Tradition from Austen to Joyce.* © 1980 by the University of Chicago. University of Chicago Press, 1980.

tolerance, love between men and women, the dialectical workings of social institutions and history, and humor itself.

I

Trollope, like Thackeray, thought of himself as a "weekday preacher" ("the novelist," he said, "if he have a conscience, must preach his sermons with the same purpose as the clergyman, and must have his own system of ethics"), and he found his humor in the "preachers" and the milieu of the church. His way of mastering the submerged spiritual tumult of his age and reconciling the clamoring religious strains in his society with the demands and realities of the changing Victorian world is to subsume and fuse ecclesiastical affairs, organized Christianity, and the energies of secularization into a wide comic perspective. In *Barchester Towers*, he imagines a comic reformation taking place.

For Trollope, change in personal and social life—the inevitable flux of circumstances and disruptions large and small—demands constant processes of reformation, i.e., perpetual readjustments of personality and behavior and continual efforts at reestablishing authority and equilibrium in the fluidity of being. These processes are the stuff of his novels. His comedy of change is especially alive to the increasing will to independence of strong-minded women and to the tensions, problems, and incongruities that new female assertiveness and ambition cause when they clash with conventional notions about feminine decorum and "a woman's place." *Barchester Towers* shows us both private and social reformations in the relationships between the sexes happening against the setting of the church, that bastion of male primacy.

Trollope's fiction is so understated and his narrative voice so unassuming that we need to keep in mind just how important his material is. In *Barchester* and its short predecessor, *The Warden*, he creates a religious, provincial society that has to adapt itself to the world's accelerating rate of change and secularizing thrust and find ways of retaining and developing its moral values, its continuity, its harmonies, and its faith. His tone is lighthearted, but it would be hard to think of a more consequential subject. It has been said that "the drama of the modern era is the decline of religion," but, more precisely, this drama lies in the reshaping and reformation of religious drives and impulses.

II

Reading Trollope's comedy of clergymen makes it easier to see in retrospect how English novelists have played with the repressions of religion and with the gaping disparity between Christian profession and the practice of nominal Christians in the world. Superficially, Fielding's Parson Adams, Goldsmith's Vicar Primrose of Wakefield, and Sterne's Yorick and Dr. Slop may have influenced *Barchester Towers*; their authors, however, do not really make fun of the workings of the church or of the ecclesiastical world, nor do they have Trollope's communal focus. There is something of Peacock's spirit of communion in the parties that highlight *Barchester*, but Trollope has a much stronger feel for the particularity of life and of history. Like Dickens, he detested and wished to expose the Pecksniffian moral tyranny in his society, but he had more interest in conserving a moral tradition and a much greater faith in institutional life.

Of the comic writers, he owes most to Austen and Thackeray. From Austen he learned to develop a comic dialectic between character and community (including the importance of dialogue in representing change) and to render the intensity of personal relationships. Like her, he realized that a community without comic imagination can be stagnant, empty, and dangerous. *Barchester Towers*, like *Emma*, offers the blessings of grace upon humanity, but that grace is a gift of the author's comic understanding, not of God.

From *Vanity Fair* he learned the comic resources of shifting perspective. *Barchester Towers* treats a subject and a variety of characters of broad significance within a limited scope. As Thackeray shrinks Napoleon into Becky and the nineteenth century into his Vanity Fair, reducing and controlling them in his comedy, so Trollope shrinks the religious controversy, church factionalism, and secularization of his age into Barset. Thackeray continually brings to bear on his world the perspectives of Christian idealism in order to satirize it. Trollope's comic dialectic absorbs absolutist Christian visions and materialist points of view into a worldly perspective and makes theological views, including *contemptus mundi* and evangelicalism, part of the historical processes of the world.

From Thackeray, also, he seems to have gotten the idea of carrying over characters from one novel to another; but what was for Thackeray a minor and casual device for reminding people of his earlier books becomes in *Barchester Towers* a major innovation in British fiction and one crucial to Trollope's vision of life as a shifting but continuous communal process. By taking the characters and the setting of *The Warden* and expanding the Barchester world, Trollope turned out to be a chief English progenitor for the countless writers since who have preserved and developed their characters and fictional communities from novel to novel, e.g., Galsworthy, Ford Madox Ford, Mann, Proust, Faulkner, Powell, Lawrence, Waugh, even Joyce and Beckett—to say nothing of the lesser legion that has spawned hundreds of sagas, series, and soap operas.

Barchester Towers, with its continuing life, reflects an urge to break through the constructions of enclosed literary forms, with their traditional endings. It shows the appeal of a fantasy life that goes on and on. Trollope creates a human comedy of developing characters who interact with their evolving community and its institutions. That comedy is social but not impersonal, and it expresses both a desire and a way of seeking for permanence in the world. Extending the fictional structure beyond the covers of a single book or the limits of a single artwork is now so commonplace that we hardly give it a thought, but it says a lot about our longings for imaginative transcendence. I think it likely that the evolution of the modern fictional series has to do with secularization and a need to supplement or replace the "other world" of religion and the figures of religious myth with another kind of enduring, institutionalized fantasy life that one can somehow identify with and find some sort of psychological solace in. If there is any truth in that idea, it would seem apt that a novel and a series that chronicle the secularizing of the church should figure prominently in extending the formal domain of fiction. "We wish," says novelist John Fowles in words that fit Trollope neatly, "to create worlds as real as, but other than the world that is." That expresses a religious impulse, but the wish would not exist in anyone who had perfect faith in God's creation of this world and the world to come.

III

The opening chapter of *Barchester* is both an overture and a précis for the comic vision and mood of the whole book. "A novel," says Trollope, "should give a picture of common life enlivened by humour." What matters most, then, is the total image of the community in action, but what gives life to the whole are the personal traits and whims of its members, set off against each other. *The Warden* centers on one man, and its first words are "The Rev. Septimus Harding"; but *Barchester Towers* is to be the story of a community: "In the latter days of July in the year 185–, a most important question was for ten days asked in the cathedral city of Barchester, and answered every hour in various ways—Who was to be the new Bishop?" The novel is set in moving time and poses a public question in the undifferentiated but various voices of the whole town. Before we read a proper name, we have the concern with social function and the sense of communal urgency.

> The death of old Dr. Grantly . . . took place exactly as the ministry of Lord ――― was going to give place to that of Lord ―――. . . .
>
> It was pretty well understood that the out-going premier had made his selection, and that if the question rested with him, the mitre would descend on the head of Archdeacon Grantly, the old bishop's son.

It is a wonderfully conceived situation; public and private life are inseparable. Trollope's artistry here is so delicate that it can easily be missed. Taking us into the mind of his ambitious archdeacon, he carefully balances the initial public question with a private question:

> The ministry were to be out within five days: his father was to be dead within—No, he rejected that view of the subject. . . .
>
> He tried to keep his mind away from the subject, but he could not. . . . He knew it must be now or never. . . . Thus he thought long and sadly, in deep silence, and then gazed at that still living face, and then at last dared to *ask himself* whether he really longed for his father's death.
>
> The effort was a salutary one, and *the question* was answered in a moment. The proud, wishful, worldly man, sank on his knees by the bedside, and taking the bishop's hand within his own, prayed eagerly that his sins might be forgiven him.
>
> (chap. 1, italics mine)

The exact nature of Grantly's answer may be ambiguous, but what then results shows how richly complex even a blunt personality can be. Trollope internalizes the principle of equivocation that animates Thackeray's world view. Grantly shows himself capable of wishing for his father's death and wishing for him not to die also. The hand that he grasps is tellingly called "the bishop's" even in the moment of the son's repentance and atonement with the father. The archdeacon longs for preferment in the church and in the same instant longs to live up to Christian principles of humility too.

Harding comes in to see his officious son-in-law praying, and he is touched. Each is moved to "fellowship," and together they witness the passing of the old bishop. The "fellowship" is real, but it doesn't last. Trollope denigrates neither the dying of the gentle bishop and the passing of his pastoral way of life nor Grantly's moment of guilt and his spiritual crisis, but he revives the comic motions of worldliness and makes them follow fast upon prayer and death:

> "You cannot but rejoice that it is over," said Mr. Harding. . . .
> But how was he to act while his father-in-law stood there holding his hand? how, without appearing unfeeling, was he to forget his father in the bishop—to overlook what he had lost, and think only of what he might possibly gain?
> "No; I suppose not," said he, at last, in answer to Mr. Harding. "We have all expected it so long."

That "it," which unwittingly encompasses both the father's death and a bishopric, shows Trollope's genius for revelation in dialogue. But just as important is the internal dialogue here. The nub of experience in this book is the comedy of people having to relate to other people unlike themselves. They must define and express their desires in the context of their professional and personal relationships with others—often incongruous others—as Grantly does here in tandem with Harding.

In the presence of death, life and the hunger pangs of ambition assert themselves, and Trollope makes it funny. The comic rhythm increases, and we move back into the public world. Grantly cajoles Harding into sending the useless telegram to the newly fallen Conservative government. Trollope shifts to the world of publicity, as various newspapers speculate on who the new bishop will be. The announcement then comes that the new Liberal government is sending Bishop Proudie down from London. Death has become an aspect of the endless corporate processes of society and a cause of the comic reformation of the Barchester community.

The narrator, at the close of the chapter, returns to the private hopes of the archdeacon, now dashed, and he tentatively sympathizes with him and his worldly ambition:

> Many will think that he was wicked to grieve for the loss of episcopal power, wicked to have coveted it, wicked even to have thought about it, in the way and at the moments he had done so.
>
> With such censures I cannot profess that I completely agree. . . . A lawyer does not sin in seeking to be a judge, or in compassing his wishes by all honest means. A young diplomat entertains a fair ambition when he looks forward to be the lord of a first-rate embassy; and a poor novelist when he attempts to rival Dickens . . . commits no fault, though he may be foolish. Sidney Smith truly said that in these recreant days we cannot expect to find the majesty of St. Paul beneath the cassock of a curate. If we look to our clergymen to be more than men, we shall probably teach ourselves to think that they are less. . . .
>
> Our archdeacon was worldly—who among us is not so?

That is the prose of a man whose heart belongs to the world and who puts faith in a career. The telling comparison of the priesthood to other professions cannot help but make the religious calling seem like any other calling. Vocation in Trollope's vision is the call of the world, and the church offers, beyond spiritual guidance, professional opportunity where one may find satisfaction, a living, and possibly distinction for oneself. Not holiness and inspiration but professional competence and humanity are the ideal qualities that emerge here for a churchman.

Notice the linkage in the passage: Grantly's emotions and wishes, which, after all, Trollope imagines, take on public significance within the world of the novel but also within the world of author and reader. The archdeacon's ambition is a subject, and so is the putative reader's response to it. Everything relates character to community, including the supposed community of readers. Grantly implicates us in Barchester, and, in a larger sense, Trollope implicates us, too, in a life made not by God but by men and women.

CORPORATE CHARACTERS AND COMMUNITY

People must be bound together. They must depend on each other.
TROLLOPE, *Doctor Thorne*

All the main characters of *Barchester Towers* are relative creatures who together create its vision of community and comic reformation. Trollope insists on the interrelatedness of life. Hope for the future and for personal happiness lie in the flourishing of social life. Imagining how people interact, how they perceive others, how they touch and change each other, how their obsessions and individuality affect their society, how their roles and activities come to be shaped and defined, how they all work together as a collectivity—that is what fascinates him in Barchester. He would later create characters of greater depth and bring readers closer to individual men and women than he does here, but he would never imagine a more resonant community.

I

When I call his people "corporate characters," I mean that he sees them as parts of a functioning whole society and also that he represents individual and communal life as formed by, and insepa- rable from, corporate organization. Not coincidentally, this comedy was written at just that time in history when the modern corporation was being developed. The church in Trollope sometimes looks as if it were the corporation of a higher agency, since its ends, though moral, are worldly. In his Palliser series and in the chronicles of Barset, Trollope understands and makes art out of two major facts of modern life: (1) Lots of people find—or try to find—success, identity, meaning, and even a kind of transcendence in the corporate structure with which they associate themselves. (2) The dominant corporate structure in a community, though itself a constantly changing entity, sets the tone and the dramatic framework for the people of that place and tends to determine their groupings and their particular destinies. (For example, the conflict in the church in the Barset novels brings Eleanor Harding both her husbands.) Whether Trollope is relating his characters to the church, Parliament, gov- ernment, or the bureaucracy, he is busy creating the epic of organization men and women.

Barchester is dominated by the institution of organized religion.

A Church of England company town, Trollope means it to be typical of an important part of the nation. Like any other institution, the church is made up of worldly and comic people of all kinds. Trollope shows how everybody, from the free-thinking Stanhopes and the old-fashioned Thornes of Ullathorne to the Barchester tradesmen and leader-writers of the London *Jupiter* (i.e., the *Times*), have a stake in Barset clerical life and the currents of ecclesiastical opinion.

He grounds the novel solidly in the religious history of its time and reflects comically the era's theological parties and strife. Slope and Mrs. Proudie represent the church's Evangelical wing; Bishop Proudie, appointed by the reforming Liberals, is a "political" bishop, willing to take orders from the government—a type very familiar in the mid-Victorian age. Grantly stands for the "high and dry" church; Dr. Arabin comes out of the Oxford Movement and champions its Anglican ideals. Even some of the particular incidents of the book had their real-life analogues; e.g., the coincidence of a falling government and a dying bishop; debates about whether cathedral services should be chanted; newspapers meddling in diocesan affairs. All of this goes to show, however, that religious affairs are part of the human comedy. For Trollope, the most important moral and religious truth—the existence of faith, hope, and charity—lies in communal life, not in theological policy or opinion.

Trollope's church is not so much a model of Anglo-Catholic faith as it is a model for displaying a secular catholic version of humanity. It loosely holds together a motley collection of mutual-interest groups and serves as the institutional body within which the maneuvering for power, influence, and security can take place. Egos shape institutions, but institutions can control and soften egoism and keep open the options and possibilities for connection between individuals. The Barchester towers express a common human idealism and give continuity to the changing scene. They are signs and physical evidence that people aspire, despite their worldly folly, to sustain and develop the moral value of their lives and of the civilization to which they belong.

II

Much of the moral equilibrium and integrity of Barchester depends on Harding, whose courtesy and innocent faith put the querulousness of the Proudies, Grantly, Slope, and the rest into perspective. He is the moral link between orthodox religion and the secularizing world—between past and future. A deferential man, Harding lacks the conventional strong qualities of a hero. The narrator, however, calls Harding "a good man," exactly what James Joyce would call Leopold Bloom, the great and ridiculous hero of his modern epic, and we can see Harding as a figure who connects the "foolish" Christian faith of Erasmus's *Praise of Folly* to Joyce's secular comic faith in *Ulysses*. Trollope uses Harding to relate his readers to *his* faith, which is based on kindness and sympathetic fellow-feeling. There is a touch of the holy fool about Harding and his innocence. He functions as a kind of conscience to Grantly, the Oxford clerics, and the public men of London, his very being reminding people that disinterested virtue *can* exist. His special qualities—mildness, patience, tact, sensitivity to others, and a positive will *not* to dictate to them—his very *harmlessness*—are the qualities that make life tolerable in any age. He brings heart to the novel and, in fact, *is* its moral heart.

But Harding is not a symbol. He works in a practical way to preserve good relations. Breaks between people, sudden ruptures of tradition, sectarian enmity, distort the corporate nature of being. He smooths the way generously for the Proudie appointment, Quiverful, to take over as the new warden, and, feeling himself too old and passive to be dean of Barchester, he convinces others that Arabin, the only other character in the novel who shows true piety, should have the office. He moderates the contentiousness of the community and helps to join its generations.

I cannot make the significance of Mr. Harding any clearer or show how necessary he is to Trollope's communal faith than by quoting William James, in *The Varieties of Religious Experience*, when he discusses modern secularizing society's view of saintly humility:

> Here saintliness has to face the charge of preserving the unfit. . . . "Resist not evil," "Love your enemies," these are saintly maxims of which men of this world find it hard to speak without impatience. . . .
>
> And yet you are sure, as I am sure, that were the world confined to . . . hard-headed, hard-hearted, and hard-fisted methods exclusively, . . . the world would be an infinitely worse place than it is now to live in. The tender

grace, not of a day that is dead, but *of a day yet to be born somehow*, with the golden rule grown natural would be cut out from the perspective of our imaginations.

(italics mine)

Without the faintly ridiculous Harding there could be no moral imagination and no hope of virtue in the emerging society of the present and the future.

III

What is so impressive about the Barchester community is the way it can include so many kinds of people and points of view. Archdeacon Grantly, Dr. Slope, and Bishop Proudie are all in their own way members of a new institutional breed, completely different from Harding. Political beings, they would be just as recognizable in pin-stripes, gray flannel, or Soviet serge as in clerical garb. Grantly is an administrator jealous for the undiminished power of his profession and, like Slope, "anxious that the world should be priest-governed"; he "really understood the *business* of bishoping" (italics mine). Eager Dr. Proudie, following the main chance, "early in life adapted himself to the views held by whigs on most theological and religious subjects." A good committeeman and amenable to "those who were really in authority," he serves the reforming governmental interests that work to bring the church under the control of the modern state. In the unscrupulous and pushy Slope, Trollope gives us a fine portrait of a climbing organizational infighter, as ruthless as any beast in the modern corporate jungle. These earthy men make a mock epic of church affairs. They also show how the collective ambitions of people in the same organization can be balanced off. Trollope uses their desires to animate the community. Ironically, what results from their corporate battle is, on the whole, good. In Barchester, corporate life keeps the individual will to power in check.

The real apostle of Evangelical thought and action is Mrs. Proudie, one of the most genuinely religious people in the novel. With her sense of moral duty, her reforming obsession, her earnest inner certitude, and her utter lack of humor, she represents that oppressive, puritanical side of religion, which just asks to be ridiculed. In her unctuous language, Trollope parodies the offensive tone of certainty that marks the smug proselyte of a "higher morality." She also stars in *Barchester Towers*'s comic version of the Samson theme. The traditional sexual roles often get reversed in the novel, and not only the bishop's wife but also the Stanhope girls, Mrs. Quiverful, Miss Thorne, Susan Grantly, and Eleanor seem to shear away strength from men. It is fitting that, in this novel of clerical life, women, for so long discriminated against and relegated to secondary status by the church, should romp like so many modern Delilahs through this ecclesiastical community.

Trollope often ridicules feminism, but it would never occur to the son of Frances Trollope that a woman is less important than a man. It is true that he does not imagine women leading successful independent lives or having identities that do not relate closely to men's. What we must also see, however, is that in Barchester he cannot imagine men leading lives of value that are not closely related to, and dependent upon, women's. Arabin can find fulfillment in his professional and private life only by marrying Eleanor and thereby relating himself to the community. Trollope puts a premium on the corporate relationship of the sexes, and that may be why he is without peer among English novelists in portraying marriage and in exploring the psychological connections between men and women, as the Palliser novels, for example, show.

IV

One thing missing from Barchester before the radical and provocative Stanhope family returns is a candid sense of the ridiculous, playing, from within the community, on its establishment figures; another is the alluring sport of sexuality. The reformation of Barset calls for both sex and comedy; by creating Signora Madeline Stanhope Vesey-Neroni, Trollope sets in motion both the mocking critical spirit and the farce of sexual attraction that the place needs. William James, expressing the conventional wisdom of the nineteenth century, says that "religious experience" must be "solemn": "For common men 'religion,' whatever more special meanings it may have, signifies always a *serious* state of mind." For Trollope, religion without joking will no longer do: it cannot properly put down pride, i.e., *Proudieness*.

Madeline, in her aggressive, witty talk and her sardonic laughter, exactly fulfills the definition and function of what George

Meredith would later describe as "the Comic Spirit": "whenever they [people] wax out of proportion, overblown, affected, pretentious, bombastical, hypocritical, pedantic . . . ; whenever it sees them self-deceived . . . drifting into vanities, congregating in absurdities . . . , plotting dementedly; whenever they are at variance with their professions; are false in humility or mined with conceit, individually, or in bulk; the Spirit . . . will look humanely malign, and cast an oblique light on them, followed by volleys of silvery laughter." This "spirit" is epitomized by a scene at Mrs. Proudie's reception, where the seductive but lame signora insists, as always, on languishing, courtesan-like, on a sofa. Mrs. Proudie, livid with raging moral prudery because her protégé, Slope, has succumbed to the siren, orders him to leave the couch.

> "Is she always like this?" said the signora. "Yes—
> always—madam," said Mrs. Proudie, returning; ". . .
> always equally adverse to impropriety of conduct of every
> description." . . . The signora couldn't follow her. . . .
> But she laughed loud, and sent the sound of it ringing
> through the lobby and down the stairs after Mrs. Proudie's
> feet. Had she been as active as Grimaldi, she could
> probably have taken no better revenge.
>
> (chap. 11)

Madeline, like Becky Sharp, excels at badinage and at playing charades with the sentimental idiocies of her time. She uses role-playing and jesting to make fun of contradictions, hidden immoralities, and unconscious motives in the world. By exposing Slope, for example, and making us realize that he is the same grubby, greedy poseur in church affairs that he is in love affairs, she lets us infer the common connection between a drive for power over moral institutions and a thwarted infatuation with sexual sin. The "proper" men of Barset flock around her couch, and there she behaves with a flamboyance that kids and even makes a mockery of sex, in much the same way, and with much the same effect, as the comedienne Mae West would later do in the movies: she stimulates and then laughs at the male libido, which prudery can never quite hide.

Trollope hints that Madeline's early life included a pregnancy and the Victorian equivalent of a shotgun wedding. An internal moral censor evidently told him that the flaunting of sex, though necessary to his story, must be punished, and he made her a cripple.

Though not fully realized, Madeline is one of the most interesting figures in the book. Trollope lavishes care on her speech and gives her, along with her brother Bertie, by far the best dialogue. She has a continually probing, iconoclastic wit. Like her nonconforming siblings, Bertie and the managerial Charlotte, she takes her living from the corporate church, which supports her, freethinker though she is. She is a daughter of the church, "one of the chapter," she says, and she strikes me as emblematic of the marriage that *Barchester Towers* accomplishes between the Anglican tradition and comedy. Like comedy, Madeline isn't quite respectable; but just because she is beyond the pale, "beyond the reach of Christian charity," as Mrs. Proudie puts it—*not serious*—she can send out the peals of laughter that Barset needs for renewing itself.

In the antiheroine, Madeline, whose repartee needles stuffed shirts and slaughters sacred cows, and the plot's heroine, Eleanor, we see that ingrained Victorian tendency to regard moral virtue as incompatible with critical, satirical intelligence in a woman. Again and again, Trollope, as he does here in *Barchester,* pays lip service to conventional notions of what a woman ought to be: obedient, pliable, the demure angel-in-the-house; a sweet, nurturing, familial creature who depends for her opinions and outlook on a man— someone who will "love, honor, and obey." In England, the ultimate sanction for this view of women's role lies in Christian doctrine and practice—in the church. Trollope wants to believe in the conventional Victorian ideal of womanhood; in fact, in novel after novel he says he does. He then goes right on, in the same books, to depict over and over the dilemmas and talk of those stifled, rebelliously witty women who fired his creative imagination. (Later in his fiction Trollope would bring virtue, humor, ambition, biting wit, intelligence, and vulnerability together in Glencora Palliser, Madame Max Goesler, Violet Effingham, Mabel Grex, and a host of other intelligent and whole figures in what is very likely the finest gallery of female characters ever created by a male novelist in English.)

What makes Trollope's conflict interesting, of course, is that it was—and is—cultural. What could and should women do in the world? The development and the integrity of the social community needed the full potential and participation of women of various talents. The changing status of women was and is one of the greatest social and personal problems of modern life, and Madeline's voice, her satire of conventional hypocrisy, and her immobile, crippled being bring it home to Barchester.

V

Madeline and her Bohemian brother Bertie don't take life seriously; they keep looking for amusement, and they work in dialectical fashion to give the Barchester world what it lacks: skepticism, flash, drama, a love of pleasure, and a touch of frivolity. Trollope stresses their good nature, but he calls them "heartless," which means, as he uses the word, that they cannot love or feel deeply. That lack distances them from us and makes them subjects as well as instruments of satire. Bertie, for example, flits idly about Europe and the Near East, dabbling in art and religion but sticking to nothing and doing no one any good. The Stanhopes look like literary ancestors of Evelyn Waugh's Bright Young People and P. G. Wodehouse's charming parasites. (That hugely famous but critically underrated antihero of twentieth-century comic fiction, Bertie Wooster, could almost be Trollope's Bertie transposed into Jeeve's company.)

Bertie shows, even as a lazy dilettante, that bohemianism can mean comic gaiety, unexpected insight, and tolerance as well as irresponsible arrogance and cultivation of the ego. Eleanor likes him because, full of candor and fun, he never professes to be moral, nor does he preach sermons at her. He acts as an agent for Trollope's subtle, but important, comic devaluing of doctrinal dispute in religion (a devaluing that implicitly means a downplaying of Christian doctrine). Clowning about comparative religion to the bishop and the Barchester clergy, he blurts such things as "I was a Jew once, myself," sapping theology of its intimidating seriousness. Creed, for him, as it has for so many others, becomes fad and entertainment. Through Bertie, Trollope expresses something that endures in the British comic tradition and, I may say, in any lively society, and that is a hedonistic longing for pleasure and jokes, for idylls of irresponsibility. Even the brains of the industrious, when they dream, enjoy fantasies of effortlessness and ambassadors from lands of milk and honey.

Trollope carefully balances the Stanhopes and their disrespectful, campy humor with another brother-and-sister pair, the anachronistic Thornes of Ullathorne. (Ullathorne, a wordplay on extreme religious conservatism, was the title of a noted reactionary Roman Catholic bishop of the day.) The Thornes—typically, Miss Thorne is much more formidable than her bachelor brother—are unashamedly reactionary and try to shut out the present by living in the past. Trollope treats them affectionately. A community, for him, is not only a gathering of people but a gathering-together of customs and mores from different times. It has temporal variety as well as human variety and stretches across years as well as land. Since it is made from the past, it must be tolerant of the past in order not to rend itself. In a rich and good culture, there must be men and women who dedicate themselves to preserving the ideals and values of other times, as do the Thornes. Trollope conceives of the Thornes, like his other characters, as typical and having communal meaning: "Such a year or two since were the Thornes," he writes, ending his slightly patronizing chapter on them. "Such, we believe, are the inhabitants of many an English country home. May it be long before their number diminishes" (chap. 22). He knew he was being nostalgic. Neither of the Thornes marries; they have no descendants. They do, however, aid in making the match between Arabin and Eleanor. They too are part of the comic reformation of Barset and the catholicity of Trollope's outlook.

VI

Trollope's Barchester world goes to church and goes to parties, but going to parties predominates, and he gives over nearly a third of his text to them. Miss Thorne's party, welcoming Mr. Arabin, and Mrs. Proudie's party, when her husband becomes bishop, are central to the novel. Barchester social life revolves about institutional appointments and relations, and that is how Trollope perceives all society, as he shows later in the Palliser novels. He is the novelist laureate of parties, and social gatherings are his forte. His parties, however, are not the gluttonous feasts of Dickens or the festive comic communions of Peacock, but the occasions when much important social business gets done: personal fate turns, relationships are rearranged, and characters and community, in signs, words, and gestures, reveal their real being. At parties men and women get a chance to talk to each other, courting takes place, sexual tension makes the blood jump, and the human comedy surges.

Trollope's comedy reads as if he were intending it to bring

about a reunion of the diverging meanings of words by which modern society organizes itself. I mean such words as "party," "company," "corporation," "union," and "class," which have been losing their connotations of mutuality and human solidarity and now often suggest partisanship, private advantage, exclusion, and even social enmity. His parties in Barchester conserve the communal relationship and the social wholeness that potentially inhere in those words. He has a tribal sense of life, and he cares about preserving some sort of corporate integrity. Failure for him means not being able to connect with others. That is why he loves to bring people together, even very disparate people, and conjoin them in what he calls the social "sports."

Barchester's whole is greater than the sum of its parts. The life in the book has an attractiveness and a worthiness that few of the characters have if we look at them separately. Most of them—like the Proudies, Slope, the Stanhopes, Grantly, and Tom Towers—are not very nice or admirable people at all, and even Arabin, Eleanor, and Harding have their glaring shortcomings. The whole cast is not much better ethically than the figures in *Vanity Fair*. And yet the life in *Barchester Towers* seems infinitely sweeter and finer than in Thackeray's novel. The reason is that Trollope finds a value, a joyousness, and an intensity in social relationship that Thackeray does not. I am not saying that Trollope's vision is better or truer or even more conducive to great comedy; but in this novel he is much more optimistic about how people complement and compensate for each other. Henry James calls Trollope's great virtue as a writer his "complete appreciation of the usual." The meaning of that praise becomes clearer if we say that Trollope had a transfiguring faith in the usual and a talent for illuminating the wonder of it. Life, for him, is energized and made diverting by the spark of human interaction, by continuing encounter with the material world, and by the knowledge that human destiny is to be part of a community.

On almost every page he manages to convey a deep and almost obsessive interest in the minutiae of the social structure and the animation of communal relationships. His careful descriptions, for instance, of the mood and talk of different people at gatherings, of movement and positioning at parties, of the surroundings at Ulla-thorne and St. Ewold's parsonage, of the nagging worries that people have about what others are thinking, of the subtle nuances of behavior in social and professional hierarchies—all contribute to the *bricolage* that builds up an elaborate, thick, personal world.

VII

The title of one of the finest chapters, "The Bishop Sits Down to Breakfast and the Dean Dies," conveys the insistent linkage that operates in the Barchester world. It begins, "The bishop of Barchester said grace over the well-spread board in the Ullathorne dining-room; and while he did so the last breath was flying from the dean of Barchester as he lay in his sick room" (chap. 38). Trollope's corporate imagination finds apparently separate pieces of information to be part of a communal system that involves the characters featured in the chapter: "When the bishop of Barchester raised his first glass of champagne to his lips, the deanship of Barchester was a good thing in the gift of the prime minister." Everything connects and ramifies, but it doesn't lose its personal meaning for the characters. The syntax here shows an intermeshing social life that seems to function smoothly, like the Newtonian universe, except that there is nothing mechanical about it. The breakfast, as it happens, will be instrumental in determining who will be the new dean, but we do not see this until much later. Trollope, as usual, however, wants to implant the idea of connection.

The body of this chapter concerns itself with what might appear to be a trivial conversation between the signora and Arabin. Actually it is a penetrating account of corporate characters in action and the fateful nature of particular social intercourse, with its strange harmonies:

> "Why, what ails you, Mr. Arabin? . . . Your friend Mr. Slope was with me a few minutes since, full of life and spirits; why don't you rival him?"
>
> . . . Mr. Arabin winced visibly from her attack, and she knew at once that he was jealous of Mr. Slope.
>
> "But I look on you and Mr. Slope as the very antipodes of men. . . . He will gain his rewards, which will be an insipid useful wife, a comfortable income, and a reputation for sanctimony. . . . You will see all this, and then—"
>
> "Well, and what then?"
>
> "Then you will begin to wish that you had done the

same. . . . Is not such the doom of all speculative men of talent?" said she. "Do they not all sit rapt as you are now. . . ?" . . .

Who was this woman that thus read the secrets of his heart. . . ? The signora went on—"The greatest mistake any man ever made is to suppose that the good things of the world are not worth the winning. . . . You try to despise these good things, but you only try; you don't succeed."

"Don't I?" said Mr. Arabin, still musing. . . .

"I ask you the question; do you succeed?"

. . . It seemed to him as though he were being interrogated by some inner spirit of his own. . . .

"Do you not as a rule think women below your notice as companions? Let us see. There is the widow Bold looking round at you from her chair this minute. What would you say to her as a companion for life?". . .

"You cross-question me rather unfairly," he replied, "and I do not know why I answer you at all. Mrs. Bold is a very beautiful woman, and as intelligent as beautiful. . . . One that would well grace any man's house."

"And you really have the effrontery to tell me this," said she; "to me, who, as you very well know, set up to be a beauty myself, . . . you really have the effrontery to tell me that Mrs. Bold is the most beautiful woman you know."

"I did not say so," said Mr. Arabin; "you are more beautiful—. . . perhaps more clever."

"Not a word further. . . ."

"But Madame Neroni, Mrs. Bold—"

"I will not hear a word about Mrs. Bold. Dread thoughts of strychnine did pass across my brain, but she is welcome to the second place."

"Her place—"

"I won't hear anything about her or her place. I am satisfied, and that is enough. But, Mr. Arabin, I am dying with hunger; beautiful and clever as I am, you know I cannot go to my food, and yet you do not bring it to me." . . .

It was quite clear that Mr. Arabin was heartily in love

with Mrs. Bold, and the signora, with very unwonted
good nature, began to turn it over in her mind whether she
could not do him a good turn.

By the end of this tête-à-tête, the comic reformation of Arabin and
of Barchester clerical society is all but assured: Madeline, this
latter-day Eve—with whose teachings, ironically, Trollope agrees—
has preached the value of the world and cleverly taught him to heed
his own longings for pleasure, the flesh, and relationship. Miss
Thorne's breakfast turns out to be an act of comic communion that
promises the renewal of Arabin's faith in worldly life and the
resurrection of the apostolic dean of Barchester in the person of
Arabin.

A comic and worldly church sponsors this scene and party, with
its happy consequences. It countenances and uses the humor of a vain
woman to further its own regenerative ends and processes. All the
characters, likable or not, function in concert to create hope and faith
for the future of the community. Even though Slope and the
Stanhopes leave Barchester in the end, they have played their parts in
its ongoing life, and they still take their living from the same
corporate body that sustains the cathedral town. It might seem,
therefore, that this church is no less wondrous, and at least as
charitable, as the church of the supernatural God.

Career and Vocation

My heart's at my office, my heart is always there—
My heart's at my office, docketing with care;
Docketing my papers, and copying all day,
My heart's at my office, though I be far away.

TROLLOPE, *The Three Clerks*

For Trollope, one of the most important goals in life is a
successful career, and a modern career, as he imagines it, is very
likely to mean a career within an institutional or professional
framework. The chance to fulfill oneself through one's vocation is as
good an opportunity to find happiness and purpose as life offers. The
idea of career is, for him, the secular concept in which the claims of
individualism and the claims of society can best be met and reconciled; culturally, I need hardly say, it is still an immensely powerful
one. Thinking in terms of career may give a wholeness to life—a

wholeness that can seem precious as belief in one's self as an immortal soul fades. It can also give a sense of permanence in this way: one may hope to contribute to, and achieve prominence in, a profession that benefits society and goes on existing though its members die. One then would be a part of something immortal though not supernatural; old Bishop Grantly, for example, dies, but his life has merged with a corporate body that keeps on living.

Ideally, a professional career could satisfy the two Victorian imperatives to do good for others and to grow rich and successful. In both the Barchester and the Palliser series, Trollope describes the interplay of vocation and career (when he comes to write his autobiography, he sets his own life down primarily as a successful writer's career, complete with payment received for his books and a professional code for novelists). Men like Harding, Grantly, Arabin, Dr. Thorne, Phineas Finn, Plantagenet Palliser, and Lord Chiltern, in their own manner, find moral dignity, usefulness, self-sufficiency, and communal responsibility in their careers.

I

Barchester Towers, as Slope, Dr. Proudie, and Grantly prove, shows the weakening, for the clergy, of the sense of vocation as a holy calling. But, it also implicitly enhances the status of other professions by showing priests as professionals and by recognizing and honoring the modern sense of vocation. Trollope's comedy dramatizes the historical change from "profession," meaning the professing of religious faith and doctrine, to "profession" connoting a significant occupational career, demanding high competence, for which one is paid.

The big trouble, however, with making career the focal point for faith and hope is that it may tend to glorify professional success at the expense of other kinds of desirable experience and lead to narrow ambition. Stress on career can also, obviously, create huge problems in the relationship between the sexes. If vocational career is what we have instead of God, so to speak, where does that leave women? For many, as Trollope so well depicts, it leaves them filled with conflicts and wanting their own careers. The successful career, in his view, must be something more than a game of king-of-the-vocational-mountain. It requires love, or some sort of emotional and affectionate binding of self to others that resembles love, and it must be a cooperative venture.

Ideally, he says, a man's career ought to include his wife and family, and a woman's career should be to attach herself to her husband and his familial interests and, by supporting him and fulfilling the traditional feminine generative and nurturing roles, find her own successful vocation. That is his normative answer to the problem of women's place. It ran counter, however, to his own deepest experience and to his sense of the tensions in the lives of talented women. He doesn't blink away the emotional turmoil that the blocked access to careers for women can cause. His own experience and his mother's made him understand the powerful appeal of a professional career—its glamor and opportunities—and the inevitable frustrations that women felt in reconciling their conventional place in society with their potential abilities and their rising ambitions.

II

In *Barchester*, the two major figures in his comic vision of career are Arabin and Mrs. Proudie. Arabin's history is a success story about achieving a balance between worldliness and idealism in vocation and life. He is the one character in the novel who combines religious dedication, professional zeal, energy, and open-minded curiosity. If Barchester is to be anything more than an amusing but trivial place, his career must bloom there. When he comes to Barset, he is an advocate for a religion that doesn't satisfy him and, it is important to see, of a kind that Trollope finds sterile. A veteran of the Oxford Movement and a skillful polemicist on matters of abstract theological dispute, he is divorced from the world and celibate. He lacks personal connection to others. We need to see exactly what happens to him. When Grantly brings him to the community to combat Slope and Proudie, he is dispirited: "He was tired of his Oxford rooms and his college life. He regarded the wife and children of his friend with something like envy. . . . The daydream of his youth was over, and at the age of forty he felt that he was not fit to work in the spirit of an apostle. He had mistaken himself, and learned his mistake when it was past remedy" (chap. 20). Trollope shows him becoming not only a happier man but a better churchman by listening to Madeline and by loving and winning Eleanor. When Harding finds his daughter is to marry Arabin, he arranges for him to become dean of Barchester, thus increasing Arabin's moral influence. Personal and professional life are necessarily connected, and a proper career is an open process of development.

One passage on his attitude toward women before coming to Barset illuminates the antifeminism of the clerical tradition out of which Arabin comes and gives us an example of what is still, fundamentally, the most influential and pervasive form of intellectual sexism: "He looked on women . . . in the same light that one sees them regarded by many Romish priests. . . . He talked to them without putting out all his powers, and listened to them without any idea that what he should hear from them could either actuate his conduct or influence his opinion" (chap. 20). He and that clerical tradition must be reformed if his career and his faith are to flourish, and, by the end, Madeline and Eleanor both act to change his conduct and opinion.

Late in the novel, Arabin complains to Eleanor, "It is the bane of my life that on important subjects I acquire no fixed opinion. I think, and think, and go on thinking; and yet my thoughts are running ever in different directions." Surety is easy, uncertainty hard; but Arabin actually expresses one of the distinguishing characteristics—I would say glories—of a pragmatic, system-wary British intellectual tradition that has grown out of the Anglican clerical heritage. "England," says Barbara Tuchman admiringly, "dislikes the definitive." Arabin is not a fully developed character like Palliser or Josiah Crawley of *The Last Chronicle of Barset,* but in him Trollope sketches out his vision of the open-minded intellectual career. Life controls and modifies doctrine and ideology. Proper thinking, like a proper career, avoids fixity and leaves open possible ways of approaching the future profitably.

All the trends and factions in the community work for the good of Arabin's career. Such diverse influences as the signora's cynicism and sexuality, Harding's quietism, Miss Thorne's feudal instincts, and Eleanor's eligibility and inheritance all combine to favor him. At the end, only half-facetiously, Oxford refers to him as an "ornament of the age," and Trollope calls him "a studious, thoughtful, hard-working man" who lives "in mutual confidence" with his wife. In Arabin, Trollope shows that vocation and faith must be joined to community; to have a successful career, we must have, quite precisely, *faith in the world*.

III

If Arabin shows the blessings of a career, Mrs. Proudie shows its possible drawbacks. Behind the stock comic figure of the virago, we see Trollope's comedy working to ridicule and restrain a woman's drive for professional career and power. Mrs. Proudie, "a would-be priestess," wants to be bishop of Barchester. At the end she is: "In the beginning . . . three or four were contending together as to who, in fact, should be bishop. . . . Each . . . now admitted . . . that Mrs. Proudie was victorious" (chap. 51). She comes across as a figure of modern comic myth inspired by social change and male anxiety; she is a caricature of militant feminism. Trollope also has another rationale in making fun of her, which runs something like this: men are tending more and more to make their goal the wielding of power in a corporate structure and turning institutional life into a competitive jungle; God forbid, for the sake of civilization, that women should do likewise.

In his burlesque of the would-be career woman, Trollope parodies male careerism and projects a comic switch on one of the common sins of male professional ambition. *She* tyrannizes over *her* mate and in her drive for power tramples on his dignity and self-esteem. She treats him, in other words, like a long-suffering hapless wife. The satire on her expresses the incipient fear of women set loose to compete, but it also contains Trollope's basic criticism of all careerists: Mrs. Proudie can't relate to others. Through her he mocks those who identify power—especially power within an institution—with success in life.

The surprising thing about Mrs. Proudie is not that she is such a ridiculous termagant but that she is so successful. Except for the brief farce of her torn dress and the lovely mockery of her by Bertie and the signora, she does *not* come out second-best. Trollope's harsh criticism of her ambition, combined with her success at getting her way, suggests that his divided feelings about his mother might have led him to purge resentment by creating the comic Mrs. Proudie. Something he says in his autobiography reveals an almost filial feeling toward her: "I have never dissevered myself from Mrs. Proudie, and still live much in company with her ghost."

In *Barchester Towers* Trollope's last words on this woman are full of odd ironies: "As for Mrs. Proudie, our prayers for her are that she may live for ever." There is a sly mockery of the efficaciousness of prayer here, and Trollope's faith in both prayer and personal immortality seem highly suspect. In *The Last Chronicle of Barset* he does kill off Mrs. Proudie, and he tells about it with relish in the autobiography. These "prayers" look like a kind of facetious joking. It is true, however, that in *Barchester Towers* there is no killing off what she represents: the growing wave of feminine assertiveness, the impulse to make a vocation of moral bullying, and the use of the insolence of office to equate personal pride with righteousness and one's authority with God's command. She lives as an inevitable part of the enduring human comedy, but Trollope controls her by imagining a comic church, broad enough to include her career and, for the social good, to support, extend, and balance the careers of Arabin, Harding, Grantly, Slope, Dr. Proudie, and all the other Barchestrians as well. The prayers are the prayers of a comic faith that can turn to laughter what is at first sight obnoxious. Prayer, then, in the career of Mrs. Proudie—and of Trollope—in essence merges with laughter.

Barchester Towers: Victory's Defeat

Andrew Wright

Barchester Towers is a comic masterpiece whose literary ancestors bear little resemblance to it. Trollope went to school to Fielding, Jane Austen, and Scott; but *Barchester Towers* is a mixture all its own, and one thing it is not is a dirge for the past, being in this respect no more nostalgic than *Tartuffe*, whose comedy, equally sharp, proceeds from a vision equally shrewd. *The Warden* focuses, as has been shown [elsewhere], on a struggle between old power and modern justice: the central figure evades defeat by an innocence both resolute and instinctive. In *Barchester Towers*, the struggle moves to the centre of the same world, and injustice will more generally prevail, though the issues are equally contradictory, and the outcome similarly fragile. Thus this most celebrated of Trollope's novels hardly seems considerable as the repository of the longing for the snows of yesteryear, especially as the indulgence in nostalgia is revealed, even exposed, in the ridiculous persons of Squire Thorne of Ullathorne and his maiden sister, who, of the two, is the more stupefyingly addicted to antique ways.

Though *Barchester Towers* is the scene of many battles, the war is lost before the first engagement, and in this as in many other senses the novel elicits risible response. On the first page of the first chapter the immediate issue is briskly presented: the old bishop is fast expiring, and the question is whether he will die before the present

---

From *Anthony Trollope: Dream and Art.* © 1983 by Andrew Wright.

government, which is also known to be at the end of its tenure, expires also. If the archdeacon is to succeed his father as bishop he must be appointed by the present Prime Minister, a Conservative like himself; on the change of government, Dr Grantly will certainly not be appointed. He does ardently want to become bishop, and he has been made to think that he will be so designated by the outgoing premier; but he does love his father, and as the contrary emotions war within his thoughts, he

> gazed at that still living face, and then at last dared to ask himself whether he really longed for his father's death. The effort was a salutory one, and the question was answered in a moment. The proud, wishful, worldly man sank on his knees by the bedside, and taking the bishop's hand within his own, prayed eagerly that his sins might be forgiven him.

This is one of the great moments in all of the Chronicles of Barsetshire, and—as many readers have observed—it sets the seal of the reader's admiration for the archdeacon: after this, he can never really be disliked again. Not that he changes: but this glimpse into one of the actualities of his nature elicits sympathy even when, after the bishop's demise, he makes haste to send a telegram to London, still hopeful that the mitre may be bestowed upon him. But the ministry has fallen already.

In a series of leisurely introductory chapters, the narrator tells of the reform of Hiram's Hospital by an Act of Parliament; the account of the provisions of the new law does not make the reader believe that much progress has been made. Then, the new bishop and his wife must be introduced, the former as a time-serving ambitious clergyman much overshadowed by his domineering and ignorant wife—there is a parallel to be observed between the status of Mr Harding and that of the bishop, the former evidently, the latter actually, helpless. Dr Proudie is said to be in a "state of vassalage." Moreover, there is another ingredient in the brew of mischief that is to be brought to the boil in Barchester: that ingredient is the Reverend Mr Slope, domestic chaplain to the bishop on the instruction of Mrs Proudie.

> Of the Rev. Mr. Slope's parentage I am not able to say much. I have heard it asserted that he is lineally descended

from that eminent physician who assisted at the birth of
Mr. T. Shandy, and that in early years he added an 'e' to his
name, for the sake of euphony as other great men have
done before him. If this be so, I presume he was christened
Obadiah, for that is his name, in commemoration of the
conflict in which his ancestor so distinguished himself.

Slope is a cartoon, but—unlike the Shandean original—he is an
ambitious and ruthless man; his intention is to be Bishop of
Barchester in all but name, and therefore sycophancy must be his
strong suit. He thus less resembles anyone in Sterne than Pecksniff.

But the extraordinary picture is not yet complete. There are also
the Reverend Dr Vesey Stanhope and his family, especially the lamed
daughter who will make the Proudies' first reception into a splendid
piece of burlesque. By the time of that reception, the reader is
thoroughly acquainted with the outer behaviour and the inner
motives of Mr Slope, of the Proudies, and also of Dr Stanhope
himself, whose unrivalled collection of dead butterflies is the symp-
tom of his misdirected industry on the shores of Lake Como, to
which he has absented himself. Besides him and the invalid daughter,
the remarkable Signora Vesey Neroni, there are the correct but idle
Mrs Vesey Stanhope, the colourless but practical elder daughter
Charlotte, and the entirely lassitudinous son Bertie, who has been so
much of a dilettante as even to have embraced, though briefly, the
tenets of Judaism.

The comedy unfolds scenically, in an unforgettable series. There
is the scene of the archdeacon at his father's deathbed. There follows
a series of scenes that are very notable: Mr Slope's sermon, Mrs
Proudie's reception, the several interviews that Mr Slope conde-
scendingly conducts, the wonderful interview of Mrs Quiverful and
Mrs Proudie when the former thinks her husband's claims to the
wardenship have been overthrown, and Mrs Proudie's scene with
Mr Slope and the bishop in which, as the chapter heading has it,
"Mrs. Proudie Wrestles and Gets a Fall." Nor is it possible to forget
the encounter of Mr Slope and Signora Vesey Neroni, in which she
elicits a declaration of love from the infatuated clergyman and then
proceeds to laugh at him with splendid scorn.

Yet the narrator is never absent, never allows the reader to
forget him. For instance, in connection with the suit of Mr Slope to

Eleanor Bold, Trollope not only shows his hand, he positively waggles it:

> To give Eleanor her due, any suspicion as to the slightest inclination on her part towards Mr. Slope was a wrong to her. She had no more idea of marrying Mr. Slope than she had of marrying the bishop; and the idea that Mr. Slope would present himself as a suitor had never occurred to her.

Again, and even more blatantly:

> But let the gentle-hearted reader be under no apprehension whatsoever. It is not destined that Eleanor shall marry Mr. Slope or Bertie Stanhope. And here, perhaps, it may be allowed to the novelist to explain his views on a very important point in the art of telling tales. He ventures to reprobate that system which goes so far to violate all proper confidence between the author and his readers, by maintaining nearly to the end of the third volume a mystery as to the fate of their favourite personage. Nay, more, and worse than this is too frequently done. Have not often the profoundest efforts of genius been used to boggle the aspirations of the reader, to raise false hopes and false fears, and to give rise to expectations which are never to be realised? Are not promises all but made of delightful horrors, in lieu of which the writer produces nothing but most commonplace realities in his final chapter? And is there not a species of deceit in this to which the honesty of the present age should lend no countenance?
>
> And what can be the worth of that solicitude which a peep into the third volume can utterly dissipate? What the value of those literary charms which are absolutely destroyed by their enjoyment? When we have once learnt what was that picture before which hung Mrs. Ratcliffe's solemn curtain, we feel no further interest about the frame or the veil.

Of this notable and often-cited passage it should be pointed out that Trollope here shows himself to be opposed to the very cheating which Henry James reprobates, but which he imputes to Trollope. For Trollope is opposed to meretricious plot-structures, to gratuitously withheld mysteries. Clearly enough, even insistently enough, Trollope's interpositions call attention to the fact that the narrator is in full control; thus the artificiality of the constructions is underscored. Moreover, he is challenging the reader to take comically his extraordinary pictures, to look at them in a different light from that of ordinary novel readers, who simply hang on suspensefully, waiting for the next episode. Trollope promises to provide suspense without ultimate mystification, and in so doing he has respectable antecedents in the playwrights, both classical and modern, whom he read with such interest and respect.

> Our doctrine is, that the author and the reader should move along together in full confidence with each other. Let the personages of the drama undergo ever so complete a comedy of errors among themselves, let the spectator never mistake the Syracusan for the Ephesian; otherwise he is one of the dupes, and the part of a dupe is never dignified.

On this passage W. P. Ker is wise. "This confidence," he says, "does not mean that the spectator knows all the story beforehand. It means that what is going on is comedy, that the mistakes and misjudgments on the stage are understood as such." It should also be observed that Trollope here urges not only respect for the integrity of the relationship between the storyteller and the story but also—though by indirection—an equal respect for the integrity of the relationship between the story and imaginative capability, what may be called the verisimilitude of the fanciful.

A further example will make a further point, this time having to do not with plot as such but with characterization, demonstrated when in *Barchester Towers* Francis Arabin is introduced, imported from Oxford by the archdeacon to do battle with the Slopes and the Proudies. He should be a more interesting character than he is allowed to show himself to be, since he is a clever man who almost followed Newman along the path to Rome, an ornament and fellow of Lazarus, the richest of the Oxford colleges, a poet and a man of letters, a pious man, a thoughtful man. But Arabin does not come sufficiently alive in *Barchester Towers* or in any of the other novels in the series to be considered a major character, probably because he is given less to say and do than are many of the others. But Trollope has a try at making him a figure of importance, drawing back, as he so often does, far enough to be calling attention to the fact that he is the sketcher of the portrait.

> It is to be regretted that no mental method of daguerreotype of photography has yet been discovered, by which the characters of men can be reduced to writing and put into grammatical language with an unerring precision of truthful description. How often does the novelist feel, ay, and the historian also, and the biographer, that he has conceived within his mind and accurately depicted on the tablet of his brain the full character and personage of a man, and that nevertheless, when he flies to pen and ink to perpetuate the portrait, his words forsake, elude, disappoint, and play the deuce with him, till at the end of a dozen pages the man described has no more resemblance to the man conceived than the sign-board at the corner of the street has to the Duke of Cambridge?

Such a remark is not a plea, as it might be from the pen of Henry James, for the seriousness of the novelist as an historian or biographer; nor is it, as so often happens when Fielding writes in this vein to the reader, a playfully contemptuous swipe at the mendacious romance-writers whom he scorns to imitate in his fictions. From Trollope this paragraph means that there is to be an effort at accuracy of representation of the character envisioned. At the same time it manifests a resistance to the perils of didacticism and also what he sees as the possibly evil consequences of mere solemnity.

Scenic mastery and narrative agility cooperate as the novel opens out to include the magnificent Thornes of Ullathorne, the squire and his sister who live so beautifully in the past—with, for the reader's delectation, such beautifully comic effect: the squire who loves genealogy and his own blood and the essayists of the eighteenth century; and hates the apostasy of Sir Robert Peel with a passion. But he is nothing to his sister, ten years his senior,

> a living caricature of all his foibles:
> She would not open a modern quarterly, did not choose to see a magazine in her drawing-room, and would not have polluted her fingers with a shred of the "Times" for any consideration. She spoke of Addison, Swift, and Steele, as though they were still living, regarded De Foe as

the best known novelist of his country, and thought of Fielding as a young but meritorious novice in the fields of romance. In poetry, she was familiar with names as late as Dryden, and had once been seduced into reading the "Rape of the Lock"; but she regarded Spenser as the purest type of her country's literature in this line. Genealogy was her favourite insanity. . . . In religion, Miss Thorne was a pure Druidess. . . . Miss Thorne went on sighing and regretting, looking back to the divine right of kings as the ruling axiom of a golden age, and cherishing, low down in the bottom of her heart of hearts a dear unmentioned wish for the restoration of some exiled Stuart. Who would deny her the luxury of her sighs, or the sweetness of her soft regrets!

The question, for all that it is rhetorical, is marked not by the usual sign of a question, but by an exclamation point, thus delicately emphasizing the exculpatory role which the narrator here plays. And Miss Thorne's *fête-champêtre,* a comic jewel in this long novel, much though it has to do with love-making, actually deals only with love *manqué* in the service of personal ambition or of an effort at temporary sovereignty. The glorious effort of Miss Thorne is to offer entertainment entirely Tudor and "every game to be played which, in a long course of reading, Miss Thorne could ascertain to have been played in the good days of Queen Elizabeth." Besides the games and the efforts at dividing the guests according to their quality, confounded by the counterefforts of Mrs Lookaloft to consort with the best people, there is the successful effort of the Signora Vesey Neroni to draw Mr Arabin and even Mr Thorne into her web, the splendid scene of Mr Slope's proposal of marriage to an ultimately embattled Eleanor Bold, and the correspondingly feeble efforts of Bertie Stanhope to induce the same Eleanor to agree to marry him and thus extricate himself from the threat of financial ruin.

Those who regard Trollope as the apologist for things as they are need to be reminded of his depiction of the highest classes at Miss Thorne's entertainment—the De Courcys and the Proudies and the various baronets bidden to the feast. They need to be reminded to look also at Mr and Miss Thorne themselves, with their utterly ridiculous pride of blood and race and place. But the latter are regarded indulgently by Trollope. It is true that he does not regard with such forgiveness the likes of Mrs Clantantram, fashionable but boring and disagreeable in her complaints at having her roquelaure bespattered, not the Countess De Courcy, whose utterly discourteous late arrival is exacerbated by her blaming the Thornes for the state of the roads.

Pure drama, then, is never Trollope's way. He never resists commentary when he regards it as necessary to establish or maintain the special fictive status which is his ultimate design. Thus when Eleanor has boxed Slope's ear for his impertinence to her at Ullathorne, Trollope comments as follows:

> And now it is to be feared that every well-bred reader of these pages will lay down the book with disgust, feeling that, after all, the heroine is unworthy of sympathy. She is a hoyden, one will say. At any rate she is not a lady, another will exclaim. I have suspected her all through, a third will declare.

So he comments also on Mr Slope's chagrin, on Bertie's efforts. In fact, as the novel moves toward the close Trollope keeps proclaiming not his "complete appreciation of reality" or "complete appreciation of the usual" (James's first and later revised sentences on Trollope) but the conventions of fiction. Trollope writes of "leavetakings in novels." They are, he says,

> as disagreeable as they are in real life; not so sad, indeed, for they want the reality of sadness; but quite as perplexing, and generally less satisfactory. What novelist . . . can impart an interest to the last chapter of his fictitious history? Promises of two children and superhuman happiness are of no avail, nor assurance of extreme respectability carried to an age far exceeding that usually allotted to mortals.

There follows a playfully rueful little essay on the ending of a novel, to the purpose of establishing as baseless in the real world the vision of which he has given the fabric. The concluding chapter begins with the following sentence: "The end of a novel, like the end of a children's dinner party, must be made up of sweetmeats and sugar-plums." Trollope is a comic writer, and no more than Shakespeare does he propose that his fiction end by asserting its own actuality, for thus might he appear to be offering prescription; and comedy evades that snare.

To regard *Barchester Towers* as benignly regressive, as the repository of the good old ways that never were, is a temptation which some readers have been unable to resist; but that the novel continues to be read so says more about the persistence of nostalgia in the human psyche than it does about Trollope's intention or achievement. Like other thinking Victorians Trollope was made uneasy by the ferment which appeared to be so large and volatile an ingredient of the years of his maturity. The elegance and order of the imaginary cathedral town have something to be said for them, but not far beneath the surface of decorum, even at Mrs Proudie's reception and at the Ullathorne *fête-champêtre,* is an unlovely struggle. And Trollope is resolutely presentational rather than apologetic. Mr Slope is a new man and most deplorable, but there is an ounce of pity for him as the reader is begged not to condemn him too roundly for being helplessly victimized by an impolitic passion for the Signora Vesey Neroni, and for being so hopelessly venal. Nor does Trollope tip the balance in favour of Ullathorne and what it stands for. There is no doubt something attractive as well as ridiculous about Monica Thorne's attachment to the past—a past which is in large part the product of her ignorant imaginings. But to locate at Ullathorne the centre of Trollope's value system is to draw a boundary around a mirage.

The Challenge of *Barchester Towers*

Robin Gilmour

When Trollope died in 1882, the *Spectator* critic R. H. Hutton took the occasion of a recent reissue of Jane Austen's novels to reflect on the differences between the rural society she had described at the start of the century and the same society as it appeared fifty years later in Trollope's novels:

> The former is, above all things, mild and unobtrusive, not reflecting the greater world at all . . . while the latter is, above all things, possessed with the sense of the aggressiveness of the outer world, of the hurry which threatens the tranquillity even of such still pools in the rapid currents of life as Hiram's Hospital at Barchester, of the rush of commercial activity, of the competitiveness of fashion, of the conflict for existence even in outlying farms and country parsonages. Miss Austen's clergy are gentlemen of such leisurely habits of mind, that even the most energetic of them suggests a spacious and sequestered life. Mr Trollope's clergy are the centres of all sorts of crowding interests, of ecclesiastical conflicts, of attacks of the press, of temptations from the great London world. . . . Everybody in Mr Trollope is more or less under pressure, swayed hither and thither by opposite attractions, assailed on this side and on that by the strategy of rivals; every-

From *Barchester Towers*. © 1983 by Robin Gilmour. Penguin, 1983.

where someone's room is more wanted than his company;
everywhere time is short.

Hutton was one of Trollope's most astute contemporary critics and
this is a characteristically perceptive observation, although it may
strike a modern reader as a rather surprising one. The idea that "time
is short" in Trollope's world is at odds with that nostalgia for a lost
haven of peace and stability which has been one sure source of his
appeal in the twentieth century. As V. S. Pritchett wrote in 1946, he
has become "one of the great air raid shelters" and Barsetshire "one
of the great Never-Never Lands of our time. It has been the normal
country to which we all aspire." And yet Hutton was surely right,
both to set Trollope in the tradition of the novel of manners
stemming from Jane Austen, and to perceive that the rural gentry he
writes about are under challenge in a way that hers are not.

The challenge comes in part from the power of London and of
metropolitan opinion, brought suddenly closer by the technological
and social innovations of the first half of the nineteenth century. The
electric telegraph, the railway, the increased power of the press—
these make their mark in the very first chapter of *Barchester Towers*.
As Hutton went on to say, "The society which in Miss Austen's tales
seems to be wholly local, though it may have a few fine connections
with the local capital, is in Mr Trollope's a great web of which
London is the centre, and some kind of London life for the most part
the motive-power." But the challenge is deeper than this; it comes
from the spirit of reform which had been sweeping across all areas of
English life since the 1820s, and had begun to threaten the institution
which more than any other held the whole network of gentry society
together: the Church of England. *Barchester Towers* is not set in a
Never-Never Land; on the contrary, it captures unforgettably a
particular phase, a significant turning point in the history of a great
national institution, and treats it with a combination of humour,
sympathy, irony and nostalgia which has made this local subject into
a universal comic drama of change.

I

The situation of the provincial Anglican clergy in the middle of
the nineteenth century was a splendid and original subject, as
Trollope must have realized when he first broached it in *The Warden*

(1855). Before this he had tried his hand at two novels of Irish life, *The Macdermots of Ballycloran* (1847) and *The Kellys and the O'Kellys* (1848), and a third work *La Vendée* (1850), in what was for him the uncongenial genre of historical romance. The Irish books have a decided interest, but in none of these three early novels does one feel that Trollope had found his true métier. It was only when he returned to England from Ireland in 1851, and started to survey the southwestern counties for the Post Office, that the idea of Barsetshire came to him, as he records in his *Autobiography*: "In the course of this job I visited Salisbury, and whilst wandering there on a mid-summer evening round the purlieus of the cathedral I conceived the story of *The Warden*—from whence came that series of novels of which Barchester, with its bishops, deans, and archdeacon, was the central site" (chap. 5). In *The Warden* Trollope found not only a highly topical subject—the use, or abuse, of charitable funds by clergymen for whom they were not originally intended—but an approach to it that was uniquely his own. He had been struck, he says in the *Autobiography*, by "two opposite evils":

> The first . . . was the possession by the Church of certain funds and endowments which had been intended for charitable purposes, but which had been allowed to become incomes for idle Church dignitaries. . . . The second . . . was its very opposite. Though I had been much struck by the injustice above described, I had also often been angered by the undeserved severity of the newspapers towards the recipients of such incomes, who could hardly be considered to be the chief sinners in the matter.
>
> (chap. 5)

The originality of Trollope's treatment lay in taking neither the reforming nor the conservative view of the abuse, but in concentrating on the reactions of the man who benefits from it. Suppose the Warden of Hiram's Hospital to be a good man who has never considered the justice or injustice of his preferment, and suppose him to be confronted by the activities of a local reformer and the accusations of the powerful *Jupiter* newspaper, how would he behave? The answer is the story of Mr Harding and his struggle to do right in a situation which he has just learned to see may possibly be wrong. It is little more than "the history of an old man's conscience," as Henry James called it, and yet the resulting novel is the first truly characteristic expression of Trollope's genius.

In *The Warden* the challenge to the quiet ways of the provincial clergy comes from without, from the London office of the *Jupiter* and what Trollope saw as the tyrannical power of the modern newspaper. In *Barchester Towers*, which he wrote from 1855 to 1856 and published in 1857, the challenge comes from within the Church as well. Here again he had struck an original seam. There had of course been many religious novels before this, novels dealing with the problems of doubt, like James Anthony Froude's *The Nemesis of Faith* (1849), and novels attacking or defending this or that party within the Church. His novelist mother, Fanny Trollope, had written one of the most partisan of these in her anti-Evangelical *The Vicar of Wrexhill* (1837). But Trollope was the first novelist to perceive the great comic subject that lay in the predicament of the Church of England, considered as an *institution*, at this point in its history. The "subject is so fresh," the reviewer in *The Times* remarked, "and the representation so vivid, that the contracted limits of the story are forgotten, and we are left to wonder that more has not long ago been made of such promising materials."

As in *The Warden* the issue is reform, although it is treated in a less intense and specific way. The background to *Barchester Towers*, largely implicit in Trollope's handling of the battle between the Grantly and Proudie factions, is the troubled state of the Established Church in a period of rapid and what now seems to us inevitable reform. Since Parliament could legislate on ecclesiastical matters, each reforming measure which gave more power and recognition to non-Anglican groups, such as the Catholic Emancipation Act of 1829 and the 1832 Reform Act, seemed to conservative High Churchmen to threaten the Anglican character of the state and, beyond that, the very independence of the Church itself. By what right (the Archdeacon Grantlys of the time asked) could an increasingly non-Anglican Parliament, composed of English and Irish Catholics, as well as Dissenters and atheistic radicals, presume to legislate for the Established Church in England and Ireland? This, the prospect of "National Apostasy" on which John Keble preached his famous Oxford sermon in 1833, when he attacked the government's plan to suppress ten Irish bishoprics, was the real origin of the Oxford Movement, and it inspired that search for ultimate spiritual authority which, pursued through the study of the early Church

Fathers and debated in the *Tracts for the Times* (hence the name Tractarian), was to lead Newman and many of his followers into the Church of Rome. At the same time the spirit of reform was at work within the Church, in the various enactments of the Ecclesiastical Commission set up by Sir Robert Peel in 1835, and in the willingness of liberal Churchmen to cooperate with the spirit of the age. Threatened from without and divided within, the mid-century Church of England might well seem to an embattled High Church-man like Dr Grantly to be at war with itself and the world.

High Church Barchester has learned to live, however reluctantly, with this era of ecclesiastical reform. What precipitates the crisis in the novel is the arrival of a Low Church bishop with his Evangelical wife and chaplain. In this Trollope was being highly topical. Although there are some features of the outgoing ministry in chapter 1 which suggest Lord Derby's short-lived Tory administration of February to December 1852, it seems clear that the new Whig ministry in the novel was suggested by that of Lord Palmerston, which came to power in February 1855. Palmerston was not a devout man himself, but his son-in-law was Lord Shaftesbury, head of the Evangelical party in the country, and the Archbishop of Canterbury was John Bird Sumner, a man of Evangelical sympathies. "The evangelicals were never triumphant," Professor Owen Chadwick observes in his study of the Victorian Church. "But there was an epoch when they were powerful; the epoch after 1855." *Barchester Towers* belongs to the start of this epoch. The almost ten years of Palmerston's rule saw an exceptionally high number of bishoprics and deaneries fall vacant—in all he had the nomination of nineteen English and Irish sees, and thirteen English deaneries—and most of them, at the suggestion of Lord Shaftesbury, went to Low Church and Evangelical clergymen. Dr Proudie is a man whose political hour has come.

The historical irony in this situation is that the Evangelicals achieved ecclesiastical power when the period of their greatest spiritual vigour had already passed. It was in the first quarter of the nineteenth century, when "serious" religion shaped individuals of the calibre of Gladstone, Macaulay, Newman and George Eliot, that Evangelicalism had achieved its great spiritual and social triumphs, such as the abolition of the slave trade in 1807. By the middle of the century they were numerically powerful—one contemporary writer reckoned that of the 18,000 clergy in the Church of England,

roughly 3,300 could be called Evangelical, against 1,000 Tractarians
(W. J. Conybeare, "Church Parties," *Edinburgh Review* 98 [1853])—
but the spiritual initiative had long since passed to the Oxford
Movement. The Palmerston bishops were distinguished neither for
great learning nor great piety, and Trollope's portrait of the Proudies
would seem to bear out the truth of Professor Chadwick's conclusion
that "those ten years of Palmerston continued to raise the authority
and lower the prestige of the evangelical party."

Although Trollope is more interested in the political than the
theological aspect of his subject (as one would expect of a novelist
who was later to write the Palliser sequence), the party labels do
involve theological positions which would have been familiar to
contemporary readers, so some brief outline of the issues at stake
may be helpful here. Bishop Proudie and his wife are both "Low
Church," but there is a distinction to be made between them. The
bishop is Low Church in the older Whig and latitudinarian sense of
being broadminded or "liberal" on doctrinal matters, his wife in the
newer and sterner Evangelical sense. He is portrayed as an oppor-
tunist without clear ecclesiastical principles who has proved politi-
cally serviceable for that reason: "He bore with the idolatry of Rome,
tolerated even the infidelity of Socinianism, and was hand in glove
with the Presbyterian Synods of Scotland and Ulster." She holds to
the Evangelical doctrines of the supreme authority of Scripture
(reinforced by her wagging forefinger) and the importance of
Sunday, or "Sabbath," observance—another topical issue because of
Evangelical-led campaigns in 1855 and 1856 to limit Sunday trading
and stop military bands in the London parks. Her approval of Mr
Slope's cathedral sermon reveals other Evangelical attitudes: the
importance attached to private judgement in religious matters and
the corresponding distrust of church music and decoration, those
"outward ceremonies" which, Mr Slope tells the congregation, "had
become all but barbarous at a time when inward conviction was
everything." Conversely, it is through their attachment to these
same "outward ceremonies" that the clergy of Barchester reveal their
High Church sympathies, for the central doctrine of the High
Church party was a belief in the corporate authority of the Church
and the redemptive power of the sacraments, in contrast to the
individualizing emphasis of Evangelicalism on private judgement,
personal conversion and justification by faith. This party has its
different shades also. When Trollope writes that "the clergymen of

the diocese of Barchester are all of the high and dry church," he means that they are the heirs of the old easy-going, gentlemanly, unenthusiastic, undogmatic Anglicanism of the eighteenth century, which still survives in the unregenerate figure of Dr Vesey Stanhope. Archdeacon Grantly has one foot in the "high and dry" camp, but his vigorous defence of Church privilege and his awareness of the ecclesiastical battles being fought in Oxford and London make him a recognizably contemporary figure, as is the Rev. Francis Arabin: the account of his spiritual struggles after Newman's departure for Rome is a representative Tractarian case-history.

II

The modern reader encountering the intensity with which these Victorian religious conflicts were fought must often feel like asking the questions Mrs Grantly puts to her husband: " 'My dear archdeacon . . . what is the use of always fighting?' " *Barchester Towers* has two different answers to offer. One is the quietism of Mr Harding, declining the deanship: " 'I may wish that I had your spirit and energy and power of combating; but I have not. Every day that is added to my life increases my wish for peace and rest.' " To which the archdeacon makes the immortal reply: " 'And where on earth can a man have peace and rest if not in a deanery?' " The other is Mr Arabin's defence of party conflict to Eleanor:

> "I never saw anything like you clergymen," said Eleanor; "you are always thinking of fighting each other."
> "Either that," said he, "or else supporting each other. The pity is that we cannot do the one without the other. But are we not here to fight? Is not ours a church militant? What is all our work but fighting, and hard fighting, if it be well done?"

If the deeper current of the novel runs with Mr Harding's "wish for peace and rest," then its comedy exploits the possibilities inherent in the idea of clergymen "fighting." When Mr Arabin asks, " 'But are we not here to fight?' " he is voicing one of the main imperatives of Victorian culture, and Trollope, by staging the fight in a cathedral town, is throwing into a comic light one of that culture's central metaphors: the battle, in particular the civil war. Thus Thomas Hughes could write in 1891 of Dr Arnold's influence on his generation at Rugby School: "I think this was our most marked characteristic, the feeling that in school and close we were training for a big fight—were in fact already engaged in it—a fight that would last all our lives" (*The Manliness of Christ*). One thinks of Dr Arnold's son Matthew, and the "ignorant armies" clashing by night at the end of "Dover Beach"; or of the "last, dim, weird battle of the west" in Tennyson's "Passing of Arthur"; or of Browning's "Prospice": "I was ever a fighter, so—one fight more. / The best and the last!" And then one turns to chapter 6 of Trollope's novel ("War") and finds that "internecine war" has broken out because of a sermon preached in an English cathedral. The issues at stake may be serious, but the comic inflation prevents us taking them seriously. When the "wars of Arabin and Slope" are compared mock-heroically to the "angers of Agamemnon and Achilles," the inevitable effect is to make them seem like the battle of the frogs and the mice.

This may be one reason why *Barchester Towers* is that rarest of achievements—a topical novel on a contentious subject which from the first seems to have aroused amusement and affection rather than controversy. That is has continued to do so is in large measure due to the way Trollope managed to universalize his clerical subject. We can read *Barchester Towers*, and profitably, as a novel about the early-Victorian Church, but behind the battles in the cathedral close and the bishop's palace there hovers a larger and more archetypal theme. It surfaces in the twelfth chapter, "Slope versus Harding," where Mr Slope so gratuitously insults the ex-warden in the name of necessary and inevitable change: " 'It is not only in Barchester that a new man is carrying out new measures, and carting away the useless rubbish of past centuries. The same thing is going on throughout the country. . . . New men, Mr Harding, are now needed.' " Here, transposed into a minor key, is the grand subject which Coleridge found in the novels of Sir Walter Scott: "the contest between the two great moving principles of social humanity; religious adherence to the past and the ancient, the desire and the admiration of permanence, on the one hand; and the passion for increase of knowledge, for truth, as the offspring of reason—in short, the mighty instincts of *progression* and *free agency*, on the other." The difference is that whereas in Scott's fiction these "mighty instincts" are usually allowed a qualified victory, in *Barchester Towers* they are thwarted. The enduring appeal of Trollope's novel is that it recognizes the forces making for change in contemporary society, but stages a comic reversal in which the reader's "desire and . . . admiration of permanence" is subtly satisfied.

III

Some light is thrown on this aspect of the novel by considering the three-volume structure of the original edition, reprinted [in the Penguin edition] for the first time. It can be seen that the threat of innovation is strongest in volume 1, as is the sense of Barsetshire (in Hutton's words) as "a great web of which London is the centre." All seems bustle and controversy, with the telegram to Downing Street, the newspaper debate about the new bishop, the arrival of the metropolitan Proudies, and the "War" which breaks out in this clerical backwater when Mr Slope preaches his calculatedly offensive sermon. The high point is the broad comedy of Mrs Proudie's reception in chapters 10 and 11, where the opposing factions come together and the she-bishop suffers her first reverse: the careering sofa which carries away her lace train, exposing the real woman beneath, is appropriately set in motion by Bertie Stanhope and contains the recumbent signora, symbolizing the comic havoc which this pair are to cause in Barchester. But it is only a temporary reverse and the remainder of the volume shows Mr Slope tightening his grip on the diocese. In volume 2 a countermovement is set up. Chapter 1 reveals Mr Arabin a man as scrupulous and unworldly as Mr Slope is unscrupulous and worldly, a comparison underlined by the difference between Arabin's quiet sermon at St Ewold's in chapter 4 and Slope's performance in the cathedral in the first volume. There is also a significant movement away from Barchester into its rural hinterland, first to the country vicarages of Plumstead and St Ewold's, and then to Ullathorne in chapter 3, where the ultracon-servative Thornes are introduced as seemingly comical survivors of a dying world. Much of the action in this volume takes place in the country, at Puddingdale and Plumstead, while in Barchester Slope starts to overreach himself and is defeated by Mrs Proudie in the battle of the bishop's bedroom in chapter 13. Volume 3 completes the reversal of the novel's initial premise that undesirable change is inevitable. The first eight chapters all take place at Ullathorne, and through the comic-feudal of the Ullathorne Sports we are asked to reexamine the Thornes and what they stand for. No longer simply absurd anachronisms, they are seen to represent the still living values of old Barsetshire and its ways: true courtesy, genuine hospitality, a quaint but genuine paternalism. Their *fête champêtre,* balancing the bishop's reception in volume 1, sees the signora—to our delight—complete the discomfiture of the newcomers begun in the earlier scene. Finally it is at Ullathorne, now established as the heartland of Barsetshire, that the awkward and not-so-young lovers are brought together by Miss Thorne. Childless themselves, the Thornes preside over the reestablishment of clerical tradition in the marriage between Mr Harding's daughter and a new High Church dean. One should not perhaps expect too symmetrical a shape from Trollope, but the organization of the three volumes does serve to highlight the process of comic reversal in the novel, the resurrection of the traditional values and kindly ways which had earlier been threatened with being carried off on Mr Slope's "rubbish cart" of history.

It could be said, however, that these values and this outcome have never been seriously threatened in *Barchester Towers.* At several points in the novel Trollope interrupts the narrative to reassure us that all will be well, as for example in the notorious passage towards the end of volume 1 when the "gentle-hearted reader" is told to be under no apprehension about the heroine's fate: "It is not destined that Eleanor shall marry Mr Slope or Bertie Stanhope." Such comments are of a piece with reminders that we are only reading a novel, with its "ordained" elements of "a male and female angel, and a male and a female devil." The final chapter opens with the cynical reflection that "the end of a novel, like the end of a children's dinner-party, must be made up of sweetmeats and sugar-plums." Henry James found these "little slaps at credulity," as he called such interruptions of the realistic illusion, "suicidal" and "pernicious." A modern reader familiar with Nabokov and Borges is likely to take a more charitable view, seeing them as evidence of a critical and self-conscious attitude to the conventions of the genre. *Barchester Towers* is a novel which offers the reader reassurance in the face of change; it is also a novel which knows that it is offering such reassurance and invites the reader's complicity in the illusion. Like many other novels by Trollope, and indeed by other Victorian novelists, *Barchester Towers* can be read on two levels. There is the conventional story of the battle for the beautiful widow's hand and fortune, with the good and the bad angels and the appropriate award of sweetmeats and sugar-plums in the final chapter; and there is another story, a more stationary study of character and situation, which has subtler satisfactions to offer. Indeed, Trollope hints at this way of reading his novel in the passage where he reveals that Eleanor is not to marry either Mr Slope or Bertie Stanhope:

> And what can be the worth of that solicitude which a peep into the third volume can utterly dissipate? What the value of those literary charms that are absolutely destroyed by their enjoyment? . . . Nay, take the third volume if you please—learn from the last pages all the results of our troubled story, and the story shall have lost none of its interest, if indeed there be any interest in it to lose.

It follows that the more interesting characters are those who are least dependent on the conventions of romantic plot-making. Eleanor is almost entirely subservient to those conventions and Trollope confesses as much in the obviously ironical opening to the chapter "Baby Worship" (vol. 1, chap. 16), or in his statement that all would have been well between the lovers at Plumstead if Eleanor "had . . . but heard the whole truth from Mr Arabin. But then where would have been my novel?" Arabin is scarcely more developed in his role of bashful lover (the account of his spiritual struggles and worldly awakening in volume 2, chapter 1, is a good deal more interesting, as we shall see). Slope is an effective villain and a splendid catalyst for some of the novel's funnier scenes, but, if the truth be told, he remains a somewhat two-dimensional character. Certainly, as a study of an evangelical clergyman he cannot stand comparison with George Eliot's Amos Barton and Edgar Tryan in the contemporaneous *Scenes of Clerical Life* (1858). In Mrs Proudie, however, in Bertie and Madeline Stanhope, and above all in Archdeacon Grantly, more complex issues are raised.

IV

Prominent among these issues is worldliness. *Barchester Towers* explores and exploits a central incongruity in its clerical subject: the Church teaches the truths of eternity but has to exist in the world of time, preaches a heavenly kingdom but must survive in an earthly one. Much of the fun in the novel comes from our perception of this incongruity in the behaviour of the characters, as the two clerical factions scheme for power. But whereas another novelist might see only hypocrisy in the discrepancy between the clergy's high destiny and their human fallibility and worldliness, Trollope is not so categorical. The description of the archdeacon at the start of the novel, for example, caught between love for his dying father and eagerness for the bishopric, achieves a fine balance of sympathy, comedy and judgement which is never lost in the subsequent presentation of the character; and like the surprising defence of clerical ambition at the end of the chapter—surprising because it challenges the reader's own double standards in expecting clergymen to be different from other men—it opens a tolerant perspective on the archdeacon's worldliness. Linked as it may be on one side to the hypocrisies of the Victorian Church, on the other it serves as a rallying-point for certain of the decencies and courtesies which make for the worth of Barsetshire. The archdeacon is generous, hospitable and a gentleman; he can afford to be, as the novel makes plain, but nonetheless these are by no means insignificant attributes to Trollope, and they go to provide some at least of the standards by which the newcomers are judged.

The offence of Mrs Proudie and Mr Slope is not so much their Low Church theology as their bad manners, in first spurning the courtesy of the archdeacon and Mr Harding when they make their visit to the palace in the fifth chapter, and then abusing the hospitality of the dean and chapter with a sermon which deliberately insults cherished cathedral practices. Mr Harding, who is the touchstone of true courtesy in the novel, puts the matter in what is for Trollope the essential perspective: " 'It can hardly be the duty of a young man rudely to assail the religious convictions of his elders in the church. Courtesy should have kept him silent, even if neither charity nor modesty could do so.' " And when Eleanor remarks that "the commands of his heavenly Master" might have a higher priority for Mr Slope, Mr Harding replies:

> "Believe me, my child, that Christian ministers are never called on by God's word to insult the convictions, or even the prejudices of their brethren; and that religion is at any rate not less susceptible of urbane and courteous conduct among men, than any other study which men may take up."

This is admittedly a rather limited view of religion; it smacks a little of what the Tractarian Hurrell Froude called the "gentleman heresy," the tendency of the Anglican Church to value urbanity more than holiness. But there is no evidence that Trollope saw it as a limitation, at least at this stage in his career. In so far as he has a religious position in *Barchester Towers*, it could be summed up in the words of an urbane clergyman of the previous generation, Sydney Smith: "The longer we live, the more we are convinced of the justice of the old saying, that an *ounce of mother wit is worth a pound of clergy*; that discretion, gentle manners, common sense, and good nature, are, in men of high ecclesiastical station, of far greater importance than the greatest skill in discriminating between sublapsarian and supralapsarian doctrines" ("Persecuting Bishops").

The Proudie party's offence against "discretion, gentle manners . . . and good nature" is made worse by their offence against the usual hierarchy: Mrs Proudie has usurped her husband's episcopal throne. The Grantly faction can cope with discourtesy but petticoat government hits them where they are weakest. As many critics have pointed out, the ostensibly male-dominated clerical world of Barchester is in fact ruled by women. Mrs Proudie runs the bishop, as Charlotte Stanhope does her father, Mrs Quiverful her husband, Miss Thorne her brother, and even, in a suitably discreet way, Mrs Grantly the archdeacon. In this world of inverted authority the imposing archdeacon is comically powerless, while Mr Slope, "powerful only over the female breast," is in his element. He is a dangerous figure in petticoat-governed Barchester because he is untouched by the fear and incomprehension of women which afflict the archdeacon and Mr Arabin. Their groundless suspicions of Eleanor, which breathe some dramatic life into the otherwise rather tedious romantic plot, serve to indicate how little they understand her. Mr Slope, on the other hand, seems to be privy to the sources of female power at the palace; his influence with Mrs Proudie clearly has a sexual element, although in the tactful manner of the Victorian novelist this is never stated, only implied in her obsessive jealousy of the signora.

It is here that the signora has a crucial part to play in the novel. Ostensibly the weakest and most vulnerable of women, her resort to the sofa almost a parody of retiring Victorian womanhood, Madeline Stanhope proves to be the most powerful of all the powerful women in the novel. Her combination of sexuality and wit is lethal, and as with the archdeacon's worldliness, a certain ambiguity in the reader's response to her conduct seems inevitable. She is heartless, cynical and unprincipled, but then, as the narrator rather plaintively asks, "Is it not a pity that people who are bright and clever should so often be exceedingly improper? and that those who are never improper should so often be dull and heavy?" It must be a very dull reader of *Barchester Towers* who cannot forgive much to the character who causes such splendid havoc at Mrs Proudie's reception, or outstares the Countess De Courcy at Ullathorne. Besides, if the signora is unconventional in her vices, her virtues are unconventional too. She is refreshingly indifferent to rank, and the effect of her impropriety is nearly always to bring out the truth hidden beneath the reticent social surface—the naked appetites of lust and ambition in Slope, the secret hunger for the good things in life in Arabin. It is easy to forget, also, how much the havoc she brings serves the cause of old Barsetshire. In terms of the Saxon-Norman antithesis which Trollope took from Scott's *Ivanhoe* and made into a comic mythology of change at the Ullathorne Sports, it is the immobile signora who is the true Saxon champion in the social lists, unhorsing the rude Norman invader De Courcy:

> The countess, who since her countess-ship commenced had been accustomed to see all eyes, not royal, ducal, or marquesal, fall before her own, paused as she went on, raised her eyebrows, and stared even harder than before. But she had now to do with one who cared little for countesses. It was, one may say, impossible for mortal man or woman to abash Madeline Neroni. She opened her large, bright, lustrous eyes wider and wider, till she seemed to be all eyes. . . . The Countess De Courcy, in spite of her thirty centuries and De Courcy Castle and the fact that Lord De Courcy was grand master of the ponies to the Prince of Wales, had not a chance with her. At first the little circlet of gold wavered in the countess's hand, then the hand shook, then the circlet fell, the countess's head tossed itself into the air, and the countess's feet shambled out to the lawn.

When Lady De Courcy then joins Mrs Proudie on the lawn the political alignment of "Norman" invaders is plain, and the "Saxon" triumph complete, for the time being at least.

The same is true of Bertie Stanhope's effect in the novel. He brings to Barchester a spirit of well-bred anarchy which is delightfully subversive of the prickly dignities of the new order. When he asks the bishop, " 'Is there much to do here, at Barchester?' " or promises on his knees to " 'fly to the looms of the fairies' " to repair Mrs Proudie's ruined dress, the blend of urbanity and bohemianism (the soft glossy beard, the sky-blue suit) is devastatingly comic. Again, as with the signora, one can overlook as one laughs the extent to which Bertie's conduct in this scene is a victory, in its own way, for the social panache and freedom from convention of the old high and dry party. The new Low Church order is unlikely to allow such eccentricity to flourish, and the High Churchmen are too entrenched in their political position to see the wisdom in Bertie's suggestion that they might " 'take a lesson from Germany.' " Fifteen years later a similar point will be made more soberly in George Eliot's *Middlemarch* by another bohemian outsider, Will Ladislaw, when he reveals that Mr Casaubon's ignorance of German scholarship has rendered his "Key to All Mythologies" redundant. But this prophetic note is lost in the general outrage at Bertie's impertinence: "There was no answering this. Dignified clergymen of sixty years of age could not condescend to discuss such a matter with a young man with such clothes and such a beard."

It is scenes and characters like these which make *Barchester Towers* the great comic novel it is—that, and the author's bias towards the comfort that lies in recurrence, as opposed to the tragic stress on the finality of loss and the need for stoicism in the face of it. "How seldom does such grief endure!" Trollope observes of Eleanor's widowhood, "how blessed is the goodness which forbids it to do so!" Grief passes, stoicism is unnatural, men and women must not make excessive demands on their limited capacities for renunciation and self-denial. "Not being favourites with the tragic muse," Trollope teaches the truths of a comic accommodation to the world as it is. The character who more than any other has to learn these truths is Mr Arabin. He is not otherwise a particularly interesting creation, but the account of his spiritual and emotional crisis in the first chapter of volume 2 is one of the finest things in the novel. A man who had aspired in early manhood to a stoical apostleship, he now finds himself at the age of forty sighing for the worldly comforts he had once so easily spurned:

> Not for wealth, in its vulgar sense, had he ever sighed; not for the enjoyment of rich things, had he ever longed; but

for the allotted share of worldly bliss, which a wife, and
children, and happy home could give him, for that usual
amount of comfort which he had ventured to reject as
unnecessary for him, he did now feel that he would have
been wiser to have searched.

Mr Arabin's discovery about himself points to what is most
individual in Trollope's vision. In an age of reform, the first two
Barsetshire novels question the moral absolutism of the reforming
temper; they speak up for the comic truth that accepting the human
fallibility involved in our need for the "usual amount of comfort"
may save us from destructive illusions about ourselves and others.
Topical as *Barchester Towers* is, this emphasis is at odds with the
strenuous, angular morality of mid-Victorian culture. In *The Mill on
the Floss* (1860) George Eliot speaks of "renunciation" as "that sad
patient loving strength which holds the clue of life," with "the
thorns . . . for ever pressing on its brow" (book 6, chap. 14). That
is the high Victorian note, but it is not Trollope's. His is rather to be
heard in Archdeacon Grantly's outburst: " 'And where on earth can
a man have peace and rest if not in a deanery?' " It is that unique
blend of comedy, worldly wisdom and nostalgia for a less hurried
past which constitutes the lasting charm of Barsetshire.

Barchester Towers
and the Charms of Imperfection

Christopher Herbert

The immediate context of the *Autobiography* passage about the love of money as a "distinctive . . . characteristic of humanity" is Trollope's discussion of the publication of *Barchester Towers*. "They who preach this doctrine [of the contempt of money] will be much offended by my theory, and by this book of mine," he declares. *Barchester Towers* is indeed the vehicle of Trollope's moral theory in the form most likely to offend the "widespread prejudice" in favor of idealization in fiction; it is also, not coincidentally, an express exercise in comedy, the first in Trollope's career and among the most significant in English in the half-century since Jane Austen. The artificiality and playfulness of comic style signal themselves continually in this novel: for example, in the interlarding of the story with allusions to and direct quotations from literary texts, particularly comic ones: *Tristram Shandy, The Comedy of Errors, The Rivals, Don Quixote, Tartuffe,* and *The Taming of the Shrew,* among others. In this way we are given continual notification of the mode to which the novel belongs—a mode distinctly skewed away from the melancholy realism of its predecessor, *The Warden.* No less explicit in its announcement of literary artifice is the dominant stylistic device of *Barchester Towers,* mock heroic ("As Achilles warmed at the sight of his armour, as Don Quixote's heart grew strong when he grasped his lance, so did Mrs. Proudie look forward to fresh laurels" [chap. 26]).

From *Trollope and Comic Pleasure.* © 1987 by the University of Chicago. University of Chicago Press, 1987.

These auguries of comic entertainment are confirmed in every aspect of Trollope's story: in its assemblage of classic comic killjoys and eccentrics, its scenes of antic pandemonium like the episode of the runaway sofa, and in its narrator's remarkable assurance at an early point in the story that the dire marriages threatening Eleanor Bold are only, as the rule of comedy demands, mock dangers not to be taken seriously. "Let the gentle-hearted reader be under no appre-hension whatsoever. It is not destined that Eleanor shall marry Mr. Slope or Bertie Stanhope" (chap. 15). Notice is almost too plainly served that we are not here in a world of potentially uncontrollable consequences like that of *The Warden*, but a regulated comic world where bad outcomes can be ruled out from the start—need to be, in fact, in order for the intended pleasures of the text to come through.

Barchester Towers embodies, too, as we briefly noticed [else-where], the central themes of comedy. Nominally the conflict between the clerical establishment of Barchester and the interlopers, the Proudies and Slope, has to do with issues of church doctrine and of liturgy—"opinions as regarded dissenters, church reform, and hebdomadal council, and such like" (chap. 5)—but in fact the two sides are deployed by Trollope as the classic polar opposites and eternal antagonists of comedy: the partisans and enemies of pleasure, the former led by Archdeacon Grantly, with his frank love of "the good things of this world" (chap. 4), the latter represented by the puritanical newcomers, the Proudies and Slope. As we noted, Trollope ties the personal and moral deformities of Slope and Mrs. Proudie closely to their unnatural suppression of their own cravings for pleasure. The same argument sheds light on the "diabolical" machinations of the voluptuous siren Madeline Vesey-Neroni, who fascinates men despite being "a poor invalid" paralyzed from the waist down and thus, as the narrator circumspectly phrases it, "debarred from the ordinary pleasures of life" (chap. 27). Her compulsive seduction of men clearly is a pathological compensation for the absence of all hope of erotic pleasure. To be cut off from pleasure in this world is to suffer almost necessarily a serious damaging of personality.

More than any other single factor, however, the comic argu-ment in *Barchester Towers* revolves around an idea of character in which sympathy flows toward human imperfection rather than toward faultless idealization. The opening scene of the novel focuses attention on just this principle with enough emphasis to make its shocking, morally provocative aspect stand out sharply. The beloved old Bishop of Barchester is dying of a "long and lingering" illness, and his son, Archdeacon Grantly, who expects to be named the new bishop providing his father dies before the imminent fall of the Conservative government, is tormented by involuntary wishes that the old man die without waste of time, and thus not cost him his chance at this promotion. The archdeacon's worldly ambition could hardly be cast in a more troubling light, even though he at last is able to drive the horrid wish from his heart: "The proud, wishful, worldly man, sank on his knees by the bedside, and taking the bishop's hand within his own, prayed eagerly that his sins might be forgiven him." Such a scene is far removed from the gaiety of the comic. But then, in a virtuoso passage of Trollope's peculiarly unobtrusive kind, the story swiftly, subtly modulates into comedy, the basis of which is the tangled mixture of human motives.

The bishop dies; the archdeacon is moved by the solemnity of the occasion and yet is desperate to communicate the news to the government without the loss of a minute. At this vital juncture (not really vital, however, for the government, unknown to the archdeacon, has already fallen) he is trapped in a ludicrous predicament: Mr. Harding seizes his hand to console him—and won't let go. The archdeacon is wild to send a telegram. "But how was he to act while his father-in-law stood there holding his hand? how, without appearing unfeeling, was he to forget his father in the bishop—to overlook what he had lost, and think only of what he might possibly gain?" We are surprised to find ourselves *laughing* at the ludicrous image, in which a complex of comic effects fuse: moral anxiety is dispelled by laughter; fit chastisement is meted out; and especially, by the establishment of the comic view (in which a personal failing like the archdeacon's almost heartless ambition is sufficiently punished by a moment of extreme embarrassment), it is intimated that even rather grievous imperfection of character is not to be condemned and not merely grudgingly forgiven, but comically enjoyed. Thanks to the alchemy of comic laughter, his ambition renders the archdeacon more appealing rather than less. The effect has a strong moral logic: the archdeacon's imperfection richly humanizes him and gives the virtues that coexist with his vices deepened poignancy at the same time, a poignancy that "all but divine men and women" can never possess. A man with no mixed motives in such circumstances, the scene hints, would be a sheer unreality or an intolerable prig.

These implications of the comic event are distinctly spelled out, then, in the final paragraphs of the chapter, where Trollope formulates the moral lesson of the episode we have just witnessed. "If we look to our clergymen to be more than men," he says, "we shall probably teach ourselves to think that they are less, and can hardly hope to raise the character of the pastor by denying to him the right to entertain the aspirations of a man." The standard of flawless perfection can only be corrupt.

This affirmation of imperfect character as the proper standard of virtue, or rather of humanity, proves to be the central theme of *Barchester Towers*, and is subsequently restated more than once. "There is nothing godlike about us," declares Mr. Arabin, referring again specifically to clergymen, though the broader reference is to his role as hero in a novel (chap. 21); "Till we can become divine," says the narrator afterwards, referring here to men and women at large, "we must be content to be human, lest in our hurry for a change we sink to something lower" (chap. 43). But more significant than these polemical statements is Trollope's rich comic dramatization of his idea throughout the novel. The archdeacon is always central to this effect. He is overbearing and crotchety, as in the subtly mock-heroic scene where he rants about the evils of round dinner tables, which suggest to his mind "something democratic and parvenue" (chap. 21); especially, he stands as an almost culpably worldly and ambitious man, and as one devoted to pleasure. The carefully designed story works, however, to turn this great vice (for a man of the cloth at least) into a saving virtue, and the hilarious effects surrounding this moral transposition express the exhilarated liberation from the oppression of "customary but unintelligent piety" that forms one of comedy's chief functions. The archdeacon's frankly worldly pleasure-loving nature is a virtue because it guarantees his immunity to the ranker kinds of intolerance, cruelty, and hypocrisy that go (as so many examples in the novel testify) with low-church fanaticism. Thus his presumed vice of worldliness is correlated throughout the novel with the fundamental goodness of character that he clearly possesses—the unmistakable sign of this being his affectionate intimacy with his father-in-law Mr. Harding, the novel's touchstone of moral integrity. We see here, again, the failure of the idea of comic laughter as necessarily destructive or humiliating: when we laugh at the archdeacon's egregious worship of Mammon we are collaborating in comedy's moral legerdemain, subscribing, that is, to the interpretation of his patent flaws as strengths in disguise, as claims on our approval.

The same comic transvaluation operates still more fully in connection with the other outsider who comes to live in Barchester, the ascetic scholar Mr. Arabin. Since he is as authentically a man of self-denying virtue as the Proudies and Slope are not, his resemblance to them as another quasi-fanatical ideologue and enemy of pleasure at first goes unnoticed. But it is precisely the function of Trollope's comedy to bring it surprisingly, even shockingly, into view, and thus to usurp the ordinary moral patterns in fiction. Arabin has made for himself a reputation as "a man always ready at a moment's notice to take up the cudgels in opposition to anything that savoured of an evangelical bearing" (chap. 20), and is imported to Barchester to play just this role in its ecclesiastical wars. His partisan combat in the name of his sectarian ideas of righteousness and his code of self-denial link him, however, to his adversaries. Trollope never states this key irony in so many words; rather, he disarms it by having the saintly Arabin undergo and succumb to the seductions of worldliness and pleasure. As the image of flawless perfection dissolves into one of ordinary carnal humanity, Arabin's standing in the novel, as the paradoxical logic of comedy dictates, is not damaged but enhanced.

Thus, this paragon who is "always in earnest" (chap. 20) enters the story bearing a guilty secret: he is sick of poverty and envies his fellow clergymen who have encircled themselves with luxurious comfort. "Surely Mr. Arabin was not a man to sigh after wealth! Of all men, his friends would have unanimously declared he was the last to do so. But how little our friends know us!" (chap. 20). Trollope is unusually emphatic in his exoneration of Arabin: the code of asceticism and unworldliness, he declares, is "an outrage on human-nature," which can only be debased and distorted by attempting to suppress its longing for "wealth and worldly comfort and happiness on earth" (chap. 20). Just how provocative Trollope means his endorsement of the illicit values of materialism and selfishness to be is shown in his choosing the morally disreputable signora to deliver, in the form of a catechism administered to the still-agonized Arabin (who has scandalized himself by admitting inwardly that his love of Eleanor is mixed with love of her fortune), the speech that sums up the novel's moral program. "The greatest mistake any man ever made is to suppose that the good things of the world are not worth the winning," she declares in a passage that ought to make clear why

Trollope's fiction seemed morally dangerous to so many contemporaries. "Why are beautiful things given to us, and luxuries and pleasant enjoyments, if they be not intended to be used?" And especially, "Why were women made beautiful if men are not to regard them?" (chap. 38). The signora is as close as Trollope comes to using in his own comedy the device, so central in comic literature, of the rascals or mockers of virtue endowed with such charm and vitality that we are obliged to share their own delight in rascality. Her exhortation to Arabin, in any case, is the liberating, magnanimous gospel of comedy, which assures us that "the ordinary pleasures of youth" (chap. 15) reproved by Mr. Slope—and the pleasures of middle age too—are not to be despised.

Arabin has to confess not only his craving for "the pleasures of the world" (chap. 3), but also his propensity for what earnest evangelicals would call lust. At the same time as he is falling in love with Eleanor, he is magnetized by the seductive signora, a married woman. Considering the severe code of sexual morality current among Trollope's public in the mid-1850s, the striking thing is the more than indulgence extended to this signal straying from virtue in Arabin. His only punishment is the finely graduated one appropriate to comedy: he is made to look amusingly foolish in his wooing, as when he suspects that Eleanor prefers the loathsome Slope to him: "Poor Mr. Arabin!—untaught, illiterate, boorish, ignorant man! That at forty years of age you should know so little of the workings of a woman's heart!" (chap. 30). In his affectionate laughter at Arabin's expense, Trollope confirms our sense that the clergyman's various failings only humanize him and make him all the worthier of sympathy and esteem. Again, this transvaluation is the special prerogative and the hallmark of comedy, which by ingrained tendency mocks the heroic, the idealized, the perfect, and in this way works to restore cheerful sympathy with ordinary defective humanity.

Trollope confirms this tactic in the benediction in the final chapter of *Barchester Towers*, where he describes, for example, Eleanor's almost excessive tendency toward Catholic liturgy: "A few high church vagaries do not, [Mrs. Grantly] thinks, sit amiss on the shoulders of a young dean's wife." Once again a failing becomes, seen in the right light, a virtue. In a less whimsical tone Trollope closes the novel with an odd eulogy of Mr. Harding that goes out of its way to deny that this half-saintly figure is to be seen as "a perfect divine," "as a hero [or] as a man to be admired and talked of"; he is merely, says the narrator, "a good man without guile." In this final disavowing of the "standard of perfection," Trollope is reminding us of the serious moral argument that his comedy has implied through-out. To aim at perfection can only lead to a distortion of humanity. From the comic point of view and from Trollope's, this is not a melancholy or disillusioned conclusion but, rather, an invigorating one that makes possible a more authentic sympathy with one's fellow men and women, and thus forms the basis not only for moral optimism but for the practice of a genuinely humane realistic fiction.

Chronology

1815	Anthony Trollope born in Bloomsbury on April 24 to an impoverished barrister and Frances Trollope, who supports the family with her prolific writing.
1822	Goes to Harrow School as a day pupil.
1827	Briefly a student at Winchester College.
1834	Becomes a clerk at the Central Post Office, London.
1841	Becomes a Postal Surveyor in Ireland.
1843	Begins his first novel, *The Macdermots of Ballycloran*.
1844	Weds Rose Heseltine, who bears him two sons, Henry (1846) and Frederick (1847).
1847	*The Macdermots of Ballycloran* published.
1848	Publishes *The Kellys and the O'Kellys*.
1850	Publishes *La Vendée*.
1851	Transferred by the Post Office to southwest England, where he begins the Barsetshire series.
1853	Returns to Ireland; promoted in 1854 to Surveyor in the Northern District of Ireland.
1855	*The Warden* published.
1857	*Barchester Towers* and *The Three Clerks* published; begins to produce novels at a furious pace.
1858	Publishes *Doctor Thorne*. Travels to Egypt and the West Indies on Postal duty.
1859	Buys Waltham House at Waltham Cross in Essex and pursues the life of a gentleman and clubman. *The Bertrams* published.
1861	*Framley Parsonage* published. In the early 1860s he meets and befriends the young American Kate Field, who later becomes a famous lecturer.
1862	Publishes *Orley Farm*.

1863   Publishes *Rachel Ray*.
1864   Publishes *The Small House at Allington*. Begins the Palliser series of novels with the publication of *Can You Forgive Her?*
1865   Publishes *Miss MacKenzie*.
1866   Publishes *The Belton Estate* and *Clergymen of the Church of England*.
1867   Publishes *The Claverings* and *The Last Chronicle of Barset*. Resigns from the Post Office as head of the Eastern district (in England), having introduced the pillar box.
1868   Stands unsuccessfully for Parliament.
1869   Publishes *Phineas Finn* and *He Knew He Was Right*.
1871   Travels to see son Frederick in Australia; visits New Zealand and the United States on this trip.
1872   Returns to England, settles in London at Montague Square.
1873   Publishes *The Eustace Diamonds*.
1874   Publishes *Phineas Redux*.
1875   Publishes *The Way We Live Now*; begins *Autobiography*.
1876   Publishes *The Prime Minister*.
1878   Publishes *Is He Popenjoy?*
1879   Publishes *Thackeray* and *An Eye for An Eye*.
1880   Publishes *The Duke's Children*. Moves to a renovated farmhouse in Hampshire.
1881   Publishes *Ayala's Angel* and *Dr. Wortle's School*.
1882   Publishes *Lord Palmerston, Marion Fay*, and *Kept in the Dark*. Dies in London, December 6.
1883   *Autobiography, The Landleaguers*, and *Mr. Scarborough's Family* published posthumously.

Contributors

HAROLD BLOOM, Sterling Professor of the Humanities at Yale University, is the author of *The Anxiety of Influence, Poetry and Repression,* and many other volumes of literary criticism. His forthcoming study, *Freud: Transference and Authority,* attempts a full-scale reading of all of Freud's major writings. A MacArthur Prize Fellow, he is general editor of five series of literary criticism published by Chelsea House. During 1987–88, he served as Charles Eliot Norton Professor of Poetry at Harvard University.

SHERMAN HAWKINS is Professor of English at Wesleyan University. He has written on Fielding, Trollope, Spenser, and Shakespeare.

HUGH L. HENNEDY is Professor of English at St. Francis College in Biddeford, Maine. He is the author of *Unity in Barsetshire.*

U. C. KNOEPFLMACHER is Professor of English at Princeton University. He is the author of *Religious Humanism and the Victorian Novel: George Eliot, Walter Pater, and Samuel Butler; Laughter and Despair: Readings in Ten Novels of the Victorian Era;* and *George Eliot's Early Novels: The Limits of Realism.*

JAMES R. KINCAID is Professor of English at the University of Colorado at Boulder. He is the author of *Tennyson's Major Poems: The Comic and Ironic Patterns* and *The Novels of Anthony Trollope.*

P. D. EDWARDS is Professor of English at the University of Queensland. His books include *Anthony Trollope: His Art and Scope* and *Some Mid-Victorian Thrillers.*

ROBERT M. POLHEMUS is Professor of English at Stanford University. He is the author of *The Changing World of Anthony Trollope* and *Comic Faith: The Great Tradition from Austen to Joyce.*

ANDREW WRIGHT is Professor of Literature at the University of California at San Diego. His books include *Jane Austen's Novels: A Study in Structure* and *Henry Fielding: Mask and Feast*.

ROBIN GILMOUR is Lecturer in English at the University of Aberdeen. He is the author of *The Idea of the Gentleman in the Victorian Novel* and a study of Thackeray's *Vanity Fair*.

CHRISTOPHER HERBERT is Associate Professor of English at Northwestern University. He has published on George Eliot, Dickens, De Quincey, and Eliza Lynn Linton. His most recent book is *Trollope and Comic Pleasure*.

Bibliography

apRoberts, Ruth. *The Moral Trollope*. Athens: Ohio University Press, 1971.

Bareham, Tony, ed. *Anthony Trollope*. New York: Barnes & Noble, 1980.

Barickman, Richard, Susan MacDonald, and Myra Stark. *Corrupt Relations: Dickens, Thackeray, Trollope, Collins, and the Victorian Sexual System*. New York: Columbia University Press, 1982.

Booth, Bradford A. *Anthony Trollope: Aspects of His Life and Art*. Bloomington: Indiana University Press, 1958.

Bowen, Elizabeth. *Anthony Trollope: A New Judgement*. New York: Oxford University Press, 1946.

Brantlinger, Patrick. *The Spirit of Reform: British Literature and Politics, 1832–1867*. Cambridge: Harvard University Press, 1977.

Briggs, Asa. *Victorian People: A Reassessment of Persons and Things 1851–1867*. London: Penguin, 1965.

Cadbury, William. "Character and the Mock Heroic in *Barchester Towers*." *Texas Studies in Literature and Language* 5 (1963–64): 509–19.

Clark, John W. *The Language and Style of Anthony Trollope*. London: André Deutsch, 1975.

Cockshut, A. O. J. *Anthony Trollope: A Critical Study*. London: Collins, 1955.

Davies, Hugh Sykes. *Trollope*. London: Longmans, 1960.

Faulkner, Karen. "Anthony Trollope's Apprenticeship." *Nineteenth-Century Fiction* 38 (1983): 161–88.

Fogle, Richard Harter. "Illusion, Point of View, and Criticism." In *The Theory of the Novel: New Essays*, edited by John Halperin, 338–52. New York: Oxford University Press, 1974.

Fredman, Alice Green. *Anthony Trollope*. New York: Columbia University Press, 1971.

Garrett, Peter K. *The Victorian Multiplot Novel: Studies in Dialogical Form*. New Haven: Yale University Press, 1980.

Gerould, Winifred G., and James T. Gerould. *A Guide to Trollope*. Princeton: Princeton University Press, 1948.

Gilmour, Robin. *The Idea of the Gentleman in the Victorian Novel*. London: Allen & Unwin, 1981.

Halperin, John. *Trollope and Politics: A Study of the Pallisers and Others*. New York: Barnes & Noble, 1977.

————, ed. *Trollope Centenary Essays.* New York: St. Martin's, 1982.

Harvey, Geoffrey. *The Art of Anthony Trollope.* New York: St. Martin's, 1980.

Hennedy, Hugh L. *Unity in Barsetshire.* The Hague: Mouton, 1971.

Herbert, Christopher. *Trollope and Comic Pleasure.* Chicago: University of Chicago Press, 1987.

James, Henry. "Anthony Trollope." In *Partial Portraits.* 1911. Reprint. Brooklyn, N.Y.: Haskell House, 1969.

Kahn, John E. "The Protean Narrator and the Case of Trollope's Barsetshire Novels." *The Journal of Narrative Technique* 10 (1980): 77–98.

Kendrick, Walter. *The Novel Machine: The Theory and Fiction of Anthony Trollope.* Baltimore: Johns Hopkins University Press, 1980.

Ker, W. P. "Anthony Trollope." In *On Modern Literature.* Oxford: Oxford University Press, 1955.

Knoepflmacher, U. C. *Laughter and Despair: Readings in Ten Novels of the Victorian Era.* Berkeley: University of California Press, 1971.

Lansbury, Coral. *The Reasonable Man: Trollope's Legal Fiction.* Princeton: Princeton University Press, 1981.

McMaster, R. D. *Trollope and the Law.* London: Macmillan, 1986.

Meckier, Jerome. "The Cant of Reform: Trollope Rewrites Dickens in *The Warden.*" *Studies in the Novel* 15 (1983): 202–23.

Miller, J. Hillis. *The Ethics of Reading.* Chicago: University of Chicago Press, 1987.

Murfin, Ross C. "The Gap in Trollope's Fiction: *The Warden* as Example." *Studies in the Novel* 14 (1982): 17–30.

Nineteenth-Century Fiction 37 (1982). Special Anthony Trollope issue.

Overton, Bill. *The Unofficial Trollope.* Sussex, U.K.: Harvester, 1982.

Polhemus, Robert M. *The Changing World of Anthony Trollope.* Berkeley: University of California Press, 1968.

Pollard, Arthur. *Anthony Trollope.* London: Routledge & Kegan Paul, 1978.

Pope-Hennessy, James. *Anthony Trollope.* London: Jonathan Cape, 1971.

Sadleir, Michael. *Trollope: A Commentary.* 1927. Reprint. London: Oxford University Press, 1961.

Saldívar, Ramón. "Trollope's *The Warden* and the Fiction of Realism." *The Journal of Narrative Technique* 11 (1981): 166–83.

Shaw, W. David. "Moral Drama in *Barchester Towers.*" *Nineteenth-Century Fiction* 19 (1964–65): 45–54.

Sibley, Gay. "The Spectrum of 'Taste' in *Barchester Towers.*" *Studies in the Novel* 17 (1985): 38–52.

Skilton, David. *Anthony Trollope and His Contemporaries: A Study in the Theory and Conventions of Mid-Victorian Fiction.* New York: St. Martin's, 1972.

Slakey, Roger. "Trollope's Case for the Moral Imperative." *Nineteenth-Century Fiction* 28 (1973): 305–20.

Smalley, Donald, ed. *Trollope: The Critical Heritage.* London: Routledge & Kegan Paul, 1969.

Snow, C. P. *Trollope: His Life and Art.* New York: Scribner's, 1975.

Stebbins, Lucy P., and Richard P. Stebbins. *The Trollopes: The Chronicle of a Writing Family.* New York: Columbia University Press, 1945.

Stevenson, Lionel. "Dickens and the Origin of *The Warden.*" *Trollopian* 2 (1947): 83–89.

Terry, R. C. *Anthony Trollope: The Artist in Hiding.* London: Macmillan, 1977.

Thale, Jerome. "The Problem of Structure in Trollope." *Nineteenth Century Fiction* 15 (1960–61): 147–57.

Wall, Stephen. "Trollope, Balzac, and the Reappearing Character." *Essays in Criticism* 25 (1975): 123–43.

Walpole, Hugh. *Anthony Trollope.* New York: Macmillan, 1928.

Weissman, Judith. "Old Maids Have Friends: The Unmarried Heroine of Trollope's Barsetshire Novels." *Women & Literature* 5, no. 1 (1977): 15–25.

West, Rebecca. *The Court and the Castle: Some Treatments of a Recurrent Theme.* New Haven: Yale University Press, 1957.

Acknowledgments

"Mr. Harding's Church Music" by Sherman Hawkins from *ELH* 29, no. 2 (June 1962), © 1962 by the Johns Hopkins University Press, Baltimore/London. Reprinted by permission of the Johns Hopkins University Press.

"*The Warden:* Novel of Vocation" by Hugh L. Hennedy from *Unity in Barsetshire* by Hugh L. Hennedy, © 1971 by Mouton & Co., N.V. Reprinted by permission.

"*Barchester Towers:* The Comedy of Change" by U. C. Knoepflmacher from *Laughter and Despair: Readings in Ten Novels of the Victorian Era* by U. C. Knoepflmacher, © 1971 by the Regents of the University of California. Reprinted by permission of the University of California Press.

"*The Warden* and *Barchester Towers:* The Pastoral Defined" (originally entitled "The Barsetshire Chronicle: *The Warden* and *Barchester Towers*: The Pastoral Defined") by James R. Kincaid from *The Novels of Anthony Trollope* by James R. Kincaid, © 1977 by Oxford University Press. Reprinted by permission.

"The Boundaries of Barset" by P. D. Edwards from *Anthony Trollope: His Art and Scope* by P. D. Edwards, © 1977 by the University of Queensland Press. Reprinted by permission of the publisher.

"Trollope's *Barchester Towers:* Comic Reformation" by Robert M. Polhemus from *Comic Faith: The Great Tradition from Austen to Joyce* by Robert M. Polhemus, © 1980 by the University of Chicago. Reprinted by permission of the University of Chicago Press.

"*Barchester Towers:* Victory's Defeat" (originally entitled "The Chronicle of Barsetshire") by Andrew Wright from *Anthony Trollope: Dream and Art* by Andrew Wright, © 1983 by Andrew Wright. Reprinted by permission of the University of Chicago Press and Macmillan Press Ltd.

"The Challenge of *Barchester Towers*" (originally entitled "Introduction") by Robin Gilmour from *Barchester Towers* by Anthony Trollope, edited with an Introduction and Notes by Robin Gilmour (Penguin Classics, 1982), Introduction © 1983 by Robin Gilmour. Reprinted by permission of Penguin Books Ltd.

"*Barchester Towers* and the Charms of Imperfection" (originally entitled "Comic Imperfection") by Christopher Herbert from *Trollope and Comic Pleasure* by Christopher Herbert, © 1987 by the University of Chicago. Reprinted by permission of the University of Chicago Press.

Index